Conflict Resolution

How to Recognize Different Communication
Styles & Effectively Manage Conflicts

Dana Williams

Table of Contents

Introduction

I f upon reading the title of this book you thought, "Finally! Someone who recognizes that people communicate differently!" you are in the right place. Unfortunately, a lot of books and resources about conflict resolution give tips and advice without really addressing the root of the problem.

The fact is that much of the conflicts we encounter in the workplace are simple misunderstandings. When two people have very different communication styles, and are only concerned with their own benefits, reaching a resolution can be difficult at best. But when you learn to recognize different communication styles and work around them, use active listening, and clearly convey solutions, you will be a natural at resolving conflict at work and at home.

This book takes a different approach to conflict resolution. To start, newcomers to the business world will be prepared with real-world examples of how conflict arises in the workplace. More seasoned businesspeople will still benefit from this book, as it takes a unique approach to conflict resolution based on clear communication rather than "winning."

Before diving into the meat of the matter, you'll learn what character traits, skills, and experiences help people be more effective in finding solutions to conflict. You'll also learn about the five different styles of communication that most people use in their workplace interactions, and how each impact difficult situations.

After learning about these styles of communication, we will dive into how to determine your own communication style and recognize those of others throughout your interactions. From there, it will be easy to see how the assertive communication style, when combined with clear thought and reasonable solutions, can resolve conflict before it ever starts.

Finally, you will be given tools and techniques that you can use in practical, real-world situations.

Ready to handle the worst of situations with ease? Let's dig in!

Chapter 1: Conflict 101

What is conflict? The traditional definition of conflict is an argument or disagreement, typically one that lasts for an extended period. But this definition is misleading when talking about workplace conflict as these situations are often much more complex.

Most workplace conflict can be divided into two categories—acute and chronic. Acute workplace conflict refers to arguments or disagreements that arise in the moment. These issues may seem to arise out of nowhere and are resolved and dismissed just as quickly. But even these acute situations usually have an underlying, long-term motivator.

Chronic workplace conflict is more in line with the traditional definition. Resentment, discrimination, contradictory communication styles, contrasting work or leadership styles, or the perception of any of these can create constant tension between colleagues that leads to argumentative outbursts and more serious inappropriate workplace behavior.

Before you can mitigate conflict in the workplace for a more appealing company culture, you must have a full understanding of what contributes to this conflict and how to recognize it in the beginning or when it's just beneath the surface.

What Contributes to Workplace Conflict

Any working environment is going to be populated with people from a wide variety of backgrounds, religions, minorities, and cultures. Everyone's unique personal history contributes to their communication style, their work or leadership style, and how they respond to situations – all of which can lead to conflict. If you want to ensure that you are not adding to the potential for workplace conflict, it is important to understand what triggers it in the first place.

Lack of Effective Communication

A lack of effective communication is one of the most common reasons for workplace conflict. When two people have clashing communication styles, it creates a barrier that contributes to conflict. Being able to approach the issue in a different way, changing the landscape of the conversation, can be an incredible asset to quickly resolving issues before they escalate. Later chapters will focus on the different communication styles and how they can be adjusted or applied in various situations to avoid or resolve conflict.

Conflicting Work or Leadership Styles

Just as people communicate differently, so too do people work in different ways. Different work styles are what make different people better for different positions within the same industry or niche. Unfortunately, when you put someone with an isolating work style in collaboration with someone of an opposing work style, it can lead to conflict as surely as clashing communication styles.

People of different leadership styles can also clash, but it is much more common for a particular leadership style to cause disagreement with someone of a particular work style. We'll get more into all of those styles and how they interrelate in a later chapter.

Cultural Misunderstandings

Although not the focus of this book, it is worth mentioning that cultural misunderstandings are also frequently responsible for workplace conflict. This does not require someone to be intentionally or blatantly discriminatory or dismissive. Often these conflicts are brought about by simple misunderstandings. Just as different backgrounds make people communicate differently, these individual backgrounds also create a diverse tapestry of cultural "norms" that may clash with your own.

What seems normal to one person could be offensive to the next. For this reason, it is very important that you work to maintain an unbiased attitude while in a working environment and be open-minded to making adjustments based on the cultural ideals of another. This is another scenario in which clear communication may prevent conflict from ever occurring.

Lack of Professionalism

There are some workplace conflicts that cannot be managed on your own and must involve human resources and/or upper management. When the root cause of conflict is sexual or emotional harassment, a hostile work environment, bullying, proselytizing, bigotry, discrimination, nepotism, or favoritism, among other such unethical issues and views, there can be no resolution without outside intervention. In many of these cases, one way or another the two conflicting people will no longer work with each other, whether through leaving the company or changing departments or locations.

Signs of Conflict in the Workplace

If you want to head off conflict before it escalates, you will need to be able to recognize it in its infancy. Sometimes signs of conflict escape notice until full-blown physical confrontations occur. It is important for everyone, from employee to President or CEO, to recognize the subtle signs of workplace conflict so that issues can be resolved before any type of harassment or confrontation occurs.

Managers should be able to assess the attitudes and collaboration efforts of teams on a frequent basis so that issues can be identified before they occur. Weekly or biweekly coaching sessions and manager meetings can help everyone stay on the same page and ensure that signs of conflict are noticed and dealt with promptly.

Signs Your Organization is in Turmoil

A company in turmoil is a perfect catalyst for creating and exacerbating workplace conflict. This often happens when there is a change in management or ownership, such as a merger of two corporations or a father passing down the family business to a new generation. But it can also happen when a company fails to create a diverse culture that promotes the well-being of all.

Regardless of the reason for a lack of cohesion among the company's employees and management, there are some definite signs that your organization is a breeding ground for conflict. These signs include:

- The development of cliques within departments or the organization as a whole

- Strange comments, out of the ordinary sentiments, or unusual language that only seems to make sense to a few
- Physical sides being formed over conference tables and other activities involving varying personnel not accustomed to working together
- Decreases in the productivity of employees, teams, or leadership
- Increase in call-outs, personal days, and/or scheduling usage of vacation time outside normal patterns
- Decreases in voluntary overtime
- Increases in disciplinary action or human resources complaints
- Frequent and blatant displays showing a lack of trust and faith in the organization or its leadership
- A sharp increase in accusations of unfair treatment
- A general lack of compatibility between core values, ethics, and beliefs of individuals within the organization and as they relate to the organization

If you happen to notice any of these signs of your employee's discontentment, you should take the situation very seriously. You might consider doing a company-wide anonymous survey to gauge what is and isn't working for your employees, as well as their general needs for success. Doing such surveys periodically can help prevent conflict from brewing.

If you're not at a management level that allows you to take action on a company-wide basis, you can do a small survey of your own subordinates or ask for their honest feedback during coaching sessions. Approaching the situation from a standpoint of coming up with solutions to meet the needs of everyone is your best approach in these matters.

Common Behavioral Signs of Oncoming Conflict

The biggest obstacle in preventing conflict is largely a matter of perception. What causes resentment in one employee may not affect another at all. That is why it is so important to be able to recognize the early warning signs of potential conflict so that issues may be addressed before reaching that level.

The best way to keep an eye on workplace morale is through frequent personal contact with all employees. This is most efficiently handled through coaching and survey programs. During such interactions, you'll easily see signs of potential unrest and be able to address them before conflict ever arises. Some of the most common, subtle signs of anger and resentment in the workplace include:

- Lying in repeated conversations, about the completion of tasks, or in recounting situations that have occurred
- Veiled threats that can just as easily be explained away as they could be taken seriously
- Giving someone the cold shoulder, or ignoring them completely even when they have a work-related question
- Constantly minimizing the concerns of fellow employees or managers
- Undermining another employee's work by intentionally throwing obstacles in their path
- Frequently or suddenly changing moods when encountered with a specific situation or person
- Intentionally withholding information necessary for the successful completion of a project

- Frequent call-outs, coming in late, or leaving early without reasonable cause or in direct violation of attendance policies

- Constantly complaining about other employees, policies, customers, or their position in the company

When conflict starts to rise to the surface, it can manifest in more severe ways. Some people can become bullies, exhibiting behavior that could even lead to physical confrontation. Once workplace conflict reaches this boiling point, swift action must be taken to resolve it.

It is usually pretty easy to spot a bully, especially if your company has an "open door policy" that makes employees of all levels comfortable with reporting such behavior. It is very important to recognize bullying and put a stop to it immediately. Not only can such behavior lead to confrontations, in some situations it could lead to lawsuits against the company. Some of the ways bullying presents itself in the workplace include:

- Constantly changing expectations, policies, job duties, or office environment to intentionally confuse
- Using diversion to focus unfavorable attention on someone, either by lying or by speaking the truth about a private matter
- Intentionally preventing someone from taking part in a workplace activity or important project
- Direct harassment in communications and interactions, such as taunting, insulting, or provoking in person

- Indirect harassment, such as spreading vicious gossip and/or outright lies about their personal or work life
- Taking credit for work well done while shifting blame when things go wrong
- Lying repeatedly and making promises the individual has no intention of fulfilling
- Purposefully ignoring others when spoken to, or intentionally excluding a particular individual or group from business opportunities or company activities
- Making a habit of deliberately distracting from the matter at hand to avoid consequences

You must take swift action when you first notice any signs of bullying in the workplace. Bullying can ruin a company if it goes unchecked. It lowers morale and makes it very difficult to motivate staff to meet business goals. It is worth mentioning that failing to appropriately address bullying in the workplace can easily lead to violations of employment and civil law, which can lead to expensive fines and lawsuits.

Causes of Workplace Conflict

To spot the more subtle signs of oncoming conflict, you need to be aware of the most common situations that lead to workplace conflict. Most conflicts can be avoided with effective communication or productive discourse, but when the parties do not have the same communication style, conflict avoidance can be impossible without some experience and conflict resolution know-how.

Unresolved Resentment and Bitterness

A lot of conflict is also caused by feelings of bitterness, whether justified or not. Resentment rarely resolves itself. In fact, it typically becomes more profound with the passage of time, especially if the behavior that led to those feelings continues unchecked. Within large companies and corporate environments, situations with the potential for breeding resentment happen daily.

Once more, it cannot be stressed enough that all management must be constantly vigilant in monitoring staff for signs of discontent, address them swiftly, and manage them appropriately. You should always be watching for these workplace situations that cause chronic or mounting discontent:

- Enduring public or private harassment, sexual or otherwise
- Favoritism or nepotism
- Rejection of a project or proposal
- Being passed over for a promotion the individual feels is deserved
- Constant criticisms, especially when unconstructive
- Insensitivity to individual needs
- Becoming overwhelmed with tasks due to a lack of teamwork or unreasonable demands
- Betrayal of trust, either between employer/employee or between colleagues
- Unfair treatment, or the perception of unfair treatment, especially when that treatment seems to be the reflection of bigotry and discrimination

Resentment can build gradually, or it can come as a sudden wave borne upon some perceived wrong. In either case, resentment between individuals, teams, or departments must be tackled immediately and in a way that is fair and reasonable to all parties. This usually requires third party mediation. It is rare that you will be able to resolve an individual's bitterness toward yourself without outside assistance.

Of course, some indignation is borne from the work environment itself. If you start to notice feelings of resentment flowing throughout the company, it may be necessary to reevaluate your business practices and human resources policy. Some of the factors that lead to a general air of bitterness and displeasure with an employer or work environment include:

- Unfair attendance policies and lack of flexibility
- Depersonalized workplace environment
- Lack of resources for effective execution of job duties or responsibilities
- Absentee management
- Micromanaging individuals and teams, or not allowing staff to be involved in decision making, particularly as it applies to their specific position and job duties
- Unclear job duties or responsibilities, causing tasks to be dropped and projects delayed
- Unrealistic expectations from upper management
- Ignoring employee criticism or suggestions, on any organizational level.

- Frequent omissions of resources or information required for projects not disclosed until after completion, causing the need for additional efforts

In the end, resentment always leads to conflict. It is simply a matter of how quickly. Aggressive communicators will explode from intense feelings of bitterness rather quickly, so if you aren't watchful, you may not be able to avoid such confrontations. On the other hand, passive aggressive people may wait weeks, months, or even years for resentment to build before confrontation ensues.

Unfair Treatment

Acute conflicts are often caused by the perception of unfair treatment, whether by management, other staff, customers, or vendors. There are many opportunities daily for people to feel they were treated unjustly, even in the most diverse and relaxed work environments with high quality management of all levels.

Of course, what one person feels is unfair might seem reasonable to someone else. Like many things in life, fairness is a matter of perception. However, there are some common workplace behaviors and circumstances that could be interpreted as unwarranted. Other staff can cause people to feel they are being treated unfairly by:

- Spreading rumors or otherwise sullying someone's reputation without just cause
- Displaying prejudice against someone due to their race, gender, nationality, sexuality, or other personal identifying factors

- Making offensive posts and comments that directly disparage someone's reputation, either personally or professionally

There are also some workplace conditions that can make someone feel as though they are being treated unfairly. These conditions are usually caused by unreasonable company policies or unethical management. Of course, fairness is a matter of perception and some people may feel they are being treated unjustly when the situation is truly equitable for all.

Some companies are breeding grounds for conflict due to unfair policies or disciplinary processes. These issues must be addressed on an organizational level. If you notice such discriminatory practices, bring them to the attention of those who can effect real change within the company's culture.

Some of the workplace conditions or management behaviors that can lead to feelings of bitterness from the perception of unfair treatment include:

- Passing over a qualified individual for new training, responsibilities, accounts, positions, appointments, or promotions, especially if on a regular basis and appearing to be socially discriminatory
- Demoting, transferring, or dismissing an employee without good cause or without the required unbiased disciplinary process
- Paying minorities lower wages than other employees, or discriminating against the majority in favor of a particular minority
- A tendency to fire or lay off more experienced staff with seniority to save on staff wages

It is important for everyone in the workplace to be mindful of how their decisions can be interpreted by others. As a manager, it is even more important to ensure that you are following company policy and employment law explicitly so that there can be no occasion to make accusations of wrongdoing or partisan treatment.

Additional Organizational Causes of Workplace Conflict

There are many additional situations or management actions that can lead to workplace conflict. Often conflict is caused simply by a general lack of understanding of the circumstances or work to be completed. It can also be caused by:

- Confusing or frequently changing job roles, duties, and responsibilities
- Frequent changes of staff in direct or indirect supervisory positions, leading to inconsistent performance and behavioral expectations
- Continual changes to products, services, pricing, or other information vital for performance of expected job duties
- Significant or sudden changes in pay scales or systems

And, of course, the number one reason for workplace conflict is a lack of communication. Whether the communication breakdown happens on a managerial or peer level, these misunderstandings are the most common cause of workplace conflict, hence the focus of this book on communication and work styles.

These are just a few of the reasons that anger and resentment build in the workplace. Add to that the frustration of a lack of effective communication, and you have a ticking time bomb waiting to happen. By recognizing early warning signs of discontent, you may be able to head off conflict before it ever arises.

Chapter 2: How Communication, Work, Leadership and Conflict Resolution Styles Interrelate

At some point, everyone experiences a situation in which they feel as though they are talking to a brick wall. And more often than we would like, this lack of effective communication leads to misunderstandings. Fostering feelings of frustration, misunderstandings can also lead to confrontation and workplace conflict. How people work and lead also play big roles in how everyone interacts with each other. In the end, these interactions are what determine if conflict is rampant within your organization or avoided as a matter of typical company culture.

The best way to avoid workplace conflict is to prevent it from occurring in the first place. When you put yourself in the shoes of others to understand how they work, lead, and communicate, you can effectively subvert most opposing engagements or interactions, as well as resolve conflicts when they do occur. When signs of conflict arise, effective communication can put a swift end to the issue.

What Communication Styles Are and Why They Are Important

Although everyone is unique in their own way, most people fall into one of five categories when it comes to styles of communication. We'll get into the details of these styles, including how to recognize them in yourself and others, in the next chapter. For now, suffice to say that these five styles are:

- Passive
- Passive-aggressive
- Manipulative
- Aggressive
- Assertive

Of course, there will always be those that march to the beat of their own drum and may vary in their communication style depending on the environment or situation. However, every interaction you have with another individual will be marked by one of these five communication styles. How you respond to those different styles of communication will play a large role in your ability to mitigate conflict.

What other reasons make these communication styles important to conflict resolution? When two people are not able to communicate with each other effectively, it is bound to either create or increase conflict. If two people are lingering on the same thought or argument and cannot devise another way to communicate the point, it can make both parties feel as though they are talking to a brick wall, causing tensions to mount rapidly.

Additionally, if two people of opposite communication styles are engaged in conflict, it is very unlikely that an amicable resolution will be reached without third-party involvement. Such situations are usually punctuated by an air of stubbornness from both sides of the conflict, and without an outsider to mediate and restate needs and desires in a much clearer manner there can be no lasting resolution.

While there are many tools that you can use in conflict resolution based on situation, if you do not also keep communication style in mind, you are not going to be able to mitigate confrontation successfully. You must be able to communicate with the other person in such a way that you can take control of the situation without causing offense. This cannot be done without active listening and other conflict resolution skills.

This book is focusing on communication styles because it is the most overlooked tool in the conflict resolution toolbox. And it is perhaps the most important. Without a complete understanding of the different communication styles and how to approach people using them, you will not be able to effectively manage difficult situations in or out of the workplace.

You might be asking, what is the most effective communication style to use in conflict resolution? You want to always take an assertive stance, meaning that you are firm without being aggressive. By being assertive you can stand your ground without seeming stubborn, while still giving some leeway to the other party. Assertive communicators also make the best leaders. We'll get into what assertive communication looks like in conflict situations in a later chapter.

Work and Leadership Styles and Their Importance

Just as everyone communicates in their own way, so too do people differ greatly in how they work and manage others. Understanding someone's work or leadership style can help you determine the best way to collaborate to find an effective and amicable solution. On the flip side, people with differing work and leadership styles can end up in a conflict all their own due to those very differences.

Although there are four primary work styles, an individual can be known to use more than one depending on the situation. It is best to adopt these work styles in one of two ways:

1) You should adopt a well-rounded, careful blending of all four work styles, using elements from each as the situation arises
2) You should allow your style to be fluid, adapting your work style according to the task at hand

What different work styles are called, how they are broken down, or how they are defined can vary greatly depending on the resource. This is a very versatile and ever evolving area in the study of human behavior. As such, the terminology is still in the development stage, causing quite a bit of variation across presentations. For the purposes of this discussion, the primary work styles are:

- logical and analytical
- detail- and task-oriented
- supportive and happy to take on delegated tasks
- idea-oriented, looking at the big picture

You will also notice that people have varying preferences as to how they work. Some employees work best independently, without collaborating or relying on others, while others will be the opposite, working best when cooperating with a group. Thankfully, most people work best when in proximity to others, which essentially means the best of both worlds.

Often conflict arises when someone is placed in a position that is unsuitable for them. For instance, you would not put someone with an idea-oriented work style in charge of analytical data, and you wouldn't put a logical- or detail-oriented worker in charge of general brainstorming. Putting people in the right place at the right time is half the battle to creating a diverse organizational culture that quells conflict before it ever arises.

Leadership styles can also affect how a situation or conflict plays out. For example, if you put an independent employee utilizing the logical work style under a manager using the autocratic leadership style to micromanage tasks and schedules, you are creating the perfect storm for brewing workplace conflict.

Again, this is an ever-evolving area of human behavior that is just beginning to be understood by experts and academics. You are encouraged to conduct your own internet searches into the different work and leadership styles so that you can see other ways they are being defined, especially if you need more clarification of those listed below. For the purposes of this book, the common leadership styles are:

- autocratic and micromanaging
- authoritative and not prone to compromise
- pacesetting, setting and expecting certain standards
- democratic, keeping everyone's interests in mind
- coaching by using mistakes and violations of company policy opportunities for education and improvement
- affiliative, interconnecting employees and leaders to create the most productive partnerships and collaborative projects
- laid-back, generally easy to please and get along with as long as company policies are being followed

Of course, you have some laid-back management that doesn't even care enough to ensure company policy is being followed, while you have the other extreme of micromanaging every action an employee makes. Outside those extremes, the best managers incorporate the most effective of these styles— pacesetting, coaching, and affiliative.

Conflict Resolution Styles and Their Importance

It should be easy to see at this point why conflict resolution styles are important. Whenever it's necessary to resolve conflict in the workplace, you need to carefully choose the appropriate conflict resolution style to approach that specific situation with those specific individuals and their specific communication and work styles. For example, you wouldn't approach a passive-aggressive employee with the detail-oriented, independent work style with a forceful conflict resolution approach, as the resulting conflict could be explosive.

Unlike work and leadership styles, conflict resolution styles are consistently defined. While there is some mild variation in how the following conflict resolution styles are defined or broken down, this is a very established and well-studied area of human behavior due to the impact on law enforcement and mental health professionals, among others. The common conflict resolution styles are:

- collaborating, working together to find win-win solutions
- compromising, a back and forth in which no one comes out a complete winner, creating lose-lose situations

- accommodating, in which you give in for the moment to get everyone back to work to meet a deadline or complete a project
- forceful, in which, as a supervisor or manager, you give the other individual no choice in the matter but to comply or face disciplinary action, sometimes up to dismissal

As we work through the rest of this book, keep these conflict resolution strategies in mind. It will become obvious as you move through each chapter how each conflict resolution style can be applied successfully, or to your detriment. While not all conflict resolution styles are appropriate for all situations, most leaders will find themselves using all the styles at some point as each new situation arises.

Other Important Skills and Traits for Successful Conflict Resolution

In addition to recognizing and dealing with different communication styles, you will also need some tools to shut down arguments and prevent full-scale confrontations. The following skills and traits should be well-developed by anyone anticipating being in a situation where they must resolve conflict either on their own behalf or someone else's.

Active Listening

We're going to talk **a lot** about active listening in this book. It is the most important skill available, and it is necessary to determine what communication style you are up against. Without active listening skills, you are not going to be able to negotiate or compromise your way out of a situation. In addition, consistently using conscious listening techniques will often head off the misunderstandings, confusion, and skewed perspectives that can launch a situation from troublesome to full blown conflict.

There are many books, websites, and the like that discuss active listening in-depth. We will not do so here, as the book would be much too long. The essential definition of active listening is that you are focused completely on what the other person is saying. There are some key things to keep in mind that allow you to be successful in developing this skill.

You should be listening to understand, not listening to respond.

When you are listening just because you are waiting for your turn to speak, you will miss out on the context of your response or the meat of the information being presented. If the person you are in conflict with says something that you want to respond to, but isn't finished speaking, it is natural for your mind to dwell on your response as they continue.

The problem with this is that if your mind is focused on that one response, you aren't really hearing anything else that the person has to say about the matter. That means the context of what distracted you is lost, and your response may not even be appropriate. This can further contribute to the confusion and make it more difficult to come to a resolution.

You should always defer judgment until after the speaker is finished. Doing so will allow you to formulate your rebuttal within context and in a reasonable manner. Also avoid interrupting if you do think of a rebuttal and try not to focus on that rebuttal as the conversation continues. Allow it to float from your mind or isolate the thought for further examination after the speaker is finished.

Ask questions or rephrase and repeat back.

This is extremely important, not just to active listening, but to conflict resolution specifically. To resolve a difficult situation, you must first have a complete understanding of that situation. Without active listening and asking questions for clarity, you won't have the information you need to reach a solution. Rephrasing and repeating information back to the speaker also ensures that you have understood them correctly before moving on, which is important for avoiding frustration from either party.

Focus on the speaker's body language.

Not only will focusing on the speaker's body language keep you focused on the conversation at hand, it will also give you clues as to the inner monologue and feelings of the person in front of you. "Listening" to their behavior often gives you just as much information as what your ears are actually hearing.

On the other hand, don't let their body language distract you. It can be easy to become overwhelmed with someone who has exaggerated movements and "talks with their hands." When someone is being overly expressive, it may become necessary to do the opposite and ignore their body language in favor of listening more intently to the content of their speech.

Side note: you should also make use of body language to show you are listening, such as leaning in, tilting your head in their direction, or nodding agreement and understanding. Keeping your posture open and avoiding a closed stance (like crossing your arms) is also recommended. You can also use body language to direct the conversation, either encouraging the speaker to continue or subtly suggesting they pause so you can interject.

Emotional Intelligence

Emotional intelligence refers to the ability to recognize emotions in yourself and others. If you are also able to empathize with the speaker, you will be even more effective in conflict resolution of all types. Emotional intelligence simply means that you can read people well enough to know if they are getting angry or upset. Often body language and eye movements can give clues to emotion if you have difficulty with this skill.

Utilizing emotional intelligence is key in resolving conflict. You can develop these skills through observation and mindfulness exercises, or more so through an in-depth guide to developing empathy. To use emotional intelligence in difficult situations, follow these steps:

- Make calm statements of fact, keeping your emotions and opinions to yourself
- Ask probing questions to determine how someone really feels about the situation
- Look at the situation from the other person's point of view. This is really the meat of empathy. "Walk a mile in their shoes."
- Use "I" statements to factually explain how the facts are affecting you
- Explain the outcome you are seeking with clarity and respect and be open to allowing for some flexibility in negotiations to find an equitable solution.

By keeping the discussion focused on the facts alone, you should be able to keep all emotion out of the conflict. This is usually the best way to avoid an actual verbal or physical confrontation, and it is the best way to manage conflict in an open workplace where such incidents can hardly be kept private. Still, you must also be able to pick up on the emotions of others and make them feel comfortable if you want to successfully quell difficult situations.

Patience

It is so important to be patient when resolving conflict. Most conflict stems from misunderstanding. If you and the other party are not using the same communication style and your styles are conflicting with one another, the continued miscommunication will begin to wear on a person. You must be able to maintain patience, keeping yourself calm and your tone even. Losing your patience will loosen or break your hold on the situation, and it is likely to escalate quickly from there.

Sometimes it can be difficult to get past an obstacle in a conflict due to the need to see the situation from a different perspective. If you seem stuck on a conflict and can't see it any other way, try seeking outside assistance. This is one reason it is important to have a good support system in and out of the office. Some other ways to foster patience in conflict resolution include:

- Remain completely unbiased. When you don't allow bias to enter into the equation it will help you remain patient during the conversation.
- Do not confuse the feeling of discomfort for the feeling of impatience. Sometimes the mere perception that we are acting in an impatient manner can make us feel even more so. But often this is needless, as discomfort can engender similar feelings.

- Distract yourself from feelings of impatience or restlessness by asking probing questions of the speaker to get yourself back on track.

Being able to recognize impatience before it becomes explosive is a skill that not everyone possesses. There are some ways that you can tell that you are getting impatient and may be about to make a mistake in mitigating conflict. If you allow impatience to get the best of you, things could escalate quickly to a confrontation.

As you're dealing with difficult people or circumstances, take note of these personal signs of impatience:

- Increased heart rate
- Taking shorter, faster breaths
- Being unable to concentrate on the conversation, even with great effort
- Shifting weight from foot to foot or fidgeting
- Wringing hands, clenching fists, or clenching teeth

It doesn't take long for impatience to become anger, especially if the discussion is already heated. As soon as you realize that you are becoming impatient, take a moment internally or walk away for a time so that you do not contribute to a further breakdown in communication.

Maintaining a Neutral Stance

The reason many companies today require arbitration agreements is that it is generally understood that it takes someone neutral to come to a resolution between two parties. Even if you do "take sides," you cannot let the person in front of you know that. You must maintain a neutral position, pointing out pros and cons, rights, and wrongs, from both sides. This also opens the door for effective compromise.

Optimism

A lot of people will tell you that you should be upbeat and positive when addressing conflict, but for some people being upbeat and positive during a conflict is a trigger for anger rather than being calming, as intended. However, you can be optimistic without being bubbly or overly positive.

Many people are going to be much more responsive to someone who is realistically optimistic rather than overly positive. You should always try to steer the conversation toward the good in the situation, or toward an amicable solution to the problem. At the same time, you must be realistic regarding the down side of the resolution. Otherwise, the conflict will simply resurface when expectations aren't met.

Being Naturally Open Rather than Defensive

People who are naturally defensive must consciously change their behavior to be effective communicators. When you become defensive, your communication style automatically becomes more aggressive, even if that is not your usual communication style. Create an open stance with your body language as well, avoid crossing your arms and stand in a relaxed fashion.

Chapter 3: The Primary Communication Styles Defined

If you want to effectively head off, prevent, or shut down workplace conflict, you first must be able to talk to someone on their level. To do that, you must figure out where they are coming from, what they are feeling, what they want out of the situation, and how to address their concerns without escalating the situation. While most of these things are basic conflict resolution skills, being able to communicate effectively with someone requires you to recognize their communication style and adapt to it.

Here we will get into the primary communication styles that most people fall into at some point. Even though some people are chameleons and may seem like they are using different communication styles at different times, everyone has one style that they fall into the most naturally. When faced with serious conflict, people tend to revert to their natural communication style.

To be better prepared to compromise and resolve conflict, use an assertive style to communicate effectively.

What is the Passive Communication Style?

A passive communication style is typically a sign of a more submissive individual. Stop for a moment and ask yourself the question, "Who is the office push-over?" If your mind immediately summoned the image of a colleague or subordinate, you have found the perfect example of passive communication in your interactions.

Passive communicators often feel like a doormat, but also feel powerless to change the situation for themselves. As a result, they will gradually build resentment against those who take advantage of them. This resentment can build and build and build, eventually reaching such a crescendo that explosive and sometimes violent outbursts are inevitable.

You will know you are talking to a passive communicator if they fail to speak up for themselves, frequently apologize even if there is nothing to apologize for, and/or agree to everything with a mumble or soft voice.

Other Clues that Someone has a Passive Communication Style

Sometimes a passive individual will be much more subtle, and much more careful about what they say. If they aren't constantly saying "I'm sorry" or displaying a "yes ma'am, no ma'am" attitude, they may still be passive for the most part. Here are a few more verbal signs that you are dealing with a passive person:

- Refusing to answer questions about how they feel or what they need
- Not clearly communicating their needs or opinions
- Refusing to give opinions when asked, even if it directly affects them
- Speaking with a very soft voice, and increasing volume only slightly when asked to speak up

- Frequent use of filler words such as: um, maybe, sort of, etc.

- Prefacing statements with one of uncertainty, such as "I might be wrong but—"

- Constantly putting themselves down

- Apologizing when unnecessary or the other person is in the wrong

- Can sometimes ramble on in their self-doubt

It is also important to pay close attention to body language. If someone is struggling to appear outwardly calm and confident in their speech, their body language will often give them away. Some examples of body language from a passive or submissive person include:

- Looking at the ceiling, floor, walls, objects—anything or anyone but the speaker

- Looking down at the floor when giving answers as though their opinions do not matter and should not be heard

- Slumped body posture, as though they are defeated

- Severely rigid posture, as though they are struggling to maintain control of themselves

- Signs of anxiety such as fidgeting, stuttering, or being unable to complete a thought or sentence

- "Talking with their hands," or seeming to flail their hands or arms about in unexpressed frustration

- Shifting weight from one foot to the other as though restless and ready to flee the situation at the first opportunity

The biggest issue with passive communicators is that, because they seem unable to speak up for themselves, they continue to allow others to take advantage of them while inside they are seething with growing resentment. Eventually, that resentment will come to the surface, sometimes volatilely. For that reason, passive communicators can be just as troublesome in a confrontation as aggressive communicators.

What is the Passive-Aggressive Communication Style?

"A wolf in sheep's clothing."

"You can't judge a book by its cover."

"Enemy masquerading as a friend."

We have many ways of describing a person who is trying to be someone that they are not. These individuals run rampant among our society, making it difficult to trust the behavior and outward appearance of others. And it is these individuals that can be the most difficult to deal with in a conflict.

Most people in the workplace know what is expected of successful career-minded professionals, and they strive every day to meet that cookie-cutter version of themselves. Many can maintain the charade so well that one may never know their true nature. But, for the most part, people will always show their true selves during communication, whether through body language or through speech.

The people who feel the most need to "pretend" or take on a persona unnatural to them are usually those who have traits, thoughts, or a history that they are trying to hide. Because they want to fit in and avoid rocking the boat, they will often try to be passive outwardly to avoid confrontation or a closer look at their motives.

But, even the most masterful actor cannot contain every automatic or involuntary tell or habit associated with their true personality. Your true self always shines through in subtle ways, there for anyone to see as long as they are paying attention and looking for signs.

And this is what leads to passive-aggressive behavior.

Someone who is passive-aggressive will try hard to appear submissive and accommodating, but they are truly fuming with frustration, resentment, hostility, and/or anger. Due to this internal struggle, the passive-aggressive individual will lash out with veiled threats, gaslighting, or in other confrontational ways that do not technically constitute harassment or outbursts, but is obviously meant to be such.

Other Signs of Passive-Aggressive Communicators

When a passive-aggressive person is involved in conflict, they are going to be hyper-focused on making you believe they are going to be submissive. Hence, passive-aggressive communicators are going to outwardly exhibit the same signs as a passive communication style, including:

- Refusing to answer questions about how they feel or what they need
- Not clearly communicating their needs or opinions
- Refusing to give opinions when asked, even if it directly affects them
- Speak with a very soft voice, and increases only slightly when asked to speak up

- Seems to keep losing the thread of the conversation and shows other signs of being distracted away from the conversation, usually by the situation itself

- Rendered speechless when asked direct questions, especially those relating to their own actions

However, they will also display some aggressive behavior that is bound to bubble up from under the surface. If you are being vigilant in your observations during the confrontation, as you always should be, you should notice these subtle signs of aggression. Regardless of whether you pick up on it or not, the speaker often believes they are fooling the listener with their passive behavior.

Some signs of underlying aggression in speech include:

- Excessive use of sarcasm
- Denying there is an issue even as they make something an issue
- Being intentionally disruptive to the conversation or the workplace in general, while pretending to be supportive, cooperative, and obliging
- Retaliating with subtle sabotage that cannot be proven and penalized

- Taking the content of one's speech out of context intentionally to create confusion or "turn the tables" back to their favor

Because they are intent on appearing submissive, those whose passive aggressive attitudes are most ingrained may not give any indication of their true motives through speech. It is usually much easier to identify passive aggressive people by their body language, tells, and habits, as well as some of these traits common to such communicators:

- Muttering to themselves instead of answering questions or speaking directly, refusing to speak up or clarify, then becoming upset when their needs or opinions are unmet
- Purposefully making errors in their work to delay or halt progress on collaborative projects
- Disrupting business growth through intentionally alienating important clients and accounts
- Suddenly making mistakes or being rude to customers
- Frequently calling out, coming in late, or leaving early, and becoming overly defensive when attempting to support their excuses
- Giving a constant "pity party," taking every opportunity to point out how they are being wronged
- Failing to take responsibility for mistakes and blaming others, even when they are clearly in the wrong
- Frequently derailing projects and missing deadlines, especially if they have always been prompt and helpful in the past. (Even if their excuses seem reasonable, a constant habit of such is usually intentional.)
- Being very pessimistic about everything, from career to society

When passive-aggressive communicators are challenged, they are likely to lose their temper or become extremely defensive and irate. If you must engage them in verbal confrontation, it is important that you approach them with caution, remaining firm in your position but being prepared to make accommodations to keep interactions civil.

The biggest issue with a passive-aggressive communicator is that, like passive communicators, there is rarely an indication that they are reaching the end of their fuse. They seem to simply "snap," their tempers flaring seemingly out of the blue. You may not have much warning to defuse the situation before the conflict escalates.

What is the Manipulative Communication Style?

Are you surprised to see this listed as a communication style? Most people only count four primary communication styles, but this leaves out an important element. It is unfortunate that many people are master manipulators. Their communication style, as well as their general behavior, reflects this character trait significantly.

For that reason, this book will add the manipulation communication style. It is extremely important that you can recognize and address manipulative people. Often their manipulation is so subtle that you can play right into their hands without ever knowing you have done so.

Manipulative communicators are highly observant and reactive. They will pay close attention to everything you say, both with your speech and your body language. They will then use that to react in ways that provoke you to do as they wish. Master manipulators can even make you think that what you are doing is your own idea.

Knowing if you are speaking with a manipulative person isn't always easy. If you are having a very hard time putting someone in a communication-style box, it may be that they have a manipulating communication style. Manipulating communicators are more likely to adapt their style to whatever will best serve their purposes. This makes them very hard to pin down.

Signs You are Dealing with a Manipulative Person

There are some definite warning signs that you should look for to recognize that you are dealing with someone of a manipulative personality. They will try to hide what they are doing behind charisma and distraction, which is one reason you must be observant when approaching people with an issue that could create conflict.

Some of the most obvious signs of a manipulative person are:

- They are prone to giving ultimatums
- Refusing to answer unless they get their way
- Excessive use of sarcasm
- Twisting the truth to make it look as though the facts are on their side
- Firing off facts and arguments as quickly as possible to confuse and overwhelm the listener
- Repeating the listener's name over and over again throughout the conversation
- Excessive use of irony, and perhaps use of inappropriate or dark humor
- Using humiliation to control others
- Making you question your knowledge of the facts

If someone is skilled in their manipulation, you might not be able to pinpoint the related speech easily. Everyone manipulates in their own way based on their own life experiences. However, you will have an easy time of recognizing manipulators if you pay close attention to their behavior beyond the words they speak.

You may also notice these behavioral or body language signs of manipulative communicators:

- Hand or neck rubbing to create the outward appearance of anxiety to pressure you into a decision
- Violation of personal space
- Mirroring your own body language, sometimes mockingly

- Their actions rarely match their words

- Frequently trying to cause people to feel guilty as a distraction from their own bad behavior

- Consistently taking on the role of victim instead of taking responsibility for their own part in the given conflict

- They want to take all the credit for every good outcome, and publicly

The key to dealing with a manipulative person is to recognize that you are being manipulated. Once you identify a manipulator, you can easily combat them by simply refusing to play into their schemes.

On the other hand, manipulative communicators can also escalate quickly from a mild conflict to a full-blown confrontation when confronted with their behavior. It is important to keep this in mind and to keep discussions neutral.

What is the Aggressive Communication Style?

The aggressive communication style is the one that most people watch out for, thinking that they can be the most volatile. Of course, you can see in our discussion of the communication styles thus far that all the communication styles can lead to outbursts or even physical confrontation.

The difference here is that aggressive communicators don't care about veiling their threats or trying to get along. They are only interested in what is best for them, and they are likely to do whatever it takes to get there. In the end, even though an aggressive communication style can result in conflict or confrontation, they are the easiest to deal with because they are displaying exactly how they think and feel with no thought for what anyone else thinks of them.

Because of this, you'll know right away when you're dealing with an aggressive communicator. However, keep in mind that an aggressive communicator isn't necessarily going to be verbally or physically aggressive.

The biggest problem with aggressive communicators is that they push for their own rights in a way that violates the rights of others. You will know that you are dealing with an aggressive communicator when they push hard for their own benefit and listen only to respond with their arguments.

Signs You are Dealing with an Aggressive Communicator

In addition to the signs above, you will be able to recognize right away when you are dealing with an aggressive communication style if you hear them engaging in any of these behaviors:

- Criticizing, placing blame, or otherwise attacking others
- Frequently displaying frustration with not getting their way
- Veiled or blatant threats and ultimatums
- Being outright rude
- Using "you" statements to place blame
- Refusing to admit blame or mistakes, and generally unable to admit when wrong

Aggressive communicators are also likely to show these outward behavioral signs and body language:

- "Getting in someone's face," meaning invading personal space in a threatening manner
- Impulsively storming away and then coming back with more arguments
- Using a loud and/or demanding voice during the conversation, refusing to back down even if proven wrong
- Zoning out instead of actively listening to what the other person has to say, mostly because they are uninterested in what others must say about a given situation
- Frequently interrupting the other person
- Alienating others in the workplace

Aggressive communicators aren't good at hiding their emotions, especially their anger or frustration. You'll be able to tell right away that you are in a potentially volatile situation. When dealing with aggressive communicators, it is important to tread lightly, and allow a neutral third party to mediate the conflict rather than exacerbating it by trying to remedy the situation on your own.

What is the Assertive Communication Style, and Why is it the Best Approach?

Although the word "assertive" may itself seem somewhat aggressive, the assertive communication style really isn't anything like the aggressive, passive-aggressive, or manipulative conversational styles. Instead of being staunch and aggressive, assertive communicators are firm in their beliefs and stance while still being reasonable and able to compromise with the other party.

Having an assertive communication style is of great benefit in the workplace. When you have an assertive style, you will be able to stand up for yourself while still maintaining a professional posture and composure. You will be able to offer constructive criticism rather than emotional attacks, which can lead to improved policies and outcomes.

Assertive communicators aren't doormats like passive communicators, but they are accommodating rather than shutting others down like aggressive communicators. They are also going to be able to actively listen, both to understand and to respond. They will be able to act quickly and make swift decisions, but they will do so in an amicable, rather than domineering, way.

Signs of an Assertive Communication Style

An assertive communication style is the best of both worlds, but two very assertive people can still butt heads. This communication style allows someone to stand up for themselves, state their opinions, and give rational arguments, but also in a way that is respectful rather than confrontational or aggressive. At the same time, assertive people expect to be treated fairly and get upset when other assertive people diminish their contributions or input.

Some of the things you'll notice when you're working with an assertive communicator are:

- Stating needs, emotions, and desires clearly and appropriately
- Using "I" statements to describe how a situation is affecting them
- Listening without interrupting and taking time to formulate an answer
- Standing up for themselves without infringing on the rights of others
- Tackling their share of the workload with zest and in a very timely manner
- Understanding and appreciating how teams combine their strengths to work together, and as such commonly praising coworkers and peers
- Speaking with a calm and even voice/tone

Assertive people don't try to hide their thoughts or actions from those with whom they interact. They are just as straightforward in their body language as they are in their speech. You don't have to play guessing games about what their body language might mean. The best assertive communicators have learned to speak without distracting movements from fidgeting or overly expressive hand gestures.

Some of the body language you'll see from assertive communicators includes:

- Be outwardly and inwardly in control as evidenced by exuding confidence
- Displaying good posture without being stiff or rigid
- Looking the speaker in the eye
- Moving deliberately and with a purpose, adding to context rather than distracting from it
- Standing with arms naturally at their sides in an open posture while still maintaining a firm stance with squared shoulders and stretched spine

It is always best to have an assertive communication style in the workplace, although you must be careful that your assertiveness is not misconstrued as aggressiveness. This requires the individual to make their points in a firm but unobtrusive way. When two people come to the negotiating table with the assertive communication style, they can reach equitable agreements swiftly and with little conflict.

If you know that you have a conflicting communication style and are dealing with an assertive person, your best bet is to allow them to take the lead in conflict resolution. Assertive people are best able to find amicable solutions, and they are also best able to resolve the conflict of others.

Chapter 4: Adjusting Your Conversation Style for Conflict Resolution

Conversation styles aren't just important because you will be dealing with them in the workplace, but throughout life in general. Recognizing your own communication style is extremely important. By being able to recognize communication styles in yourself and others, you will be able to adjust your style of communication and your responses to the individual in front of you in the moment.

As we previously mentioned, it is generally best to take an assertive communication style when trying to prevent or resolve conflict in the workplace. But sometimes taking the assertive "high road" isn't the best way to handle a situation with that particular person or in that particular moment. You should be very familiar with all the different communication styles and be able to switch among them with ease as the need arises.

How Conflict Management Styles Reflect Communication Styles

Different communication styles tend to come through in corresponding conflict management styles. Recognizing your conflict management style along with your communication style will give you an edge in dealing with workplace conflicts of all types and with all individuals in your organization, regardless of their own style.

As you work through the following basic descriptions of the five conflict management styles seen most often in the workplace, keep in mind that there is not any one conflict resolution style better than any other. Any of these conflict resolution strategies can be appropriate given the right situation.

What Are the Five Conflict Management Styles?

Just as there are five communication styles, there are five conflict management styles. The important thing to remember here is that each individual situation has its own circumstances, and not all can be treated the same way. Although it is always best to collaborate with involved parties to find a lasting solution, that isn't always possible. Being flexible in conflict resolution is vital to success.

For most, the conflict management styles they take on most frequently closely reflect their corresponding natural communication styles, but that doesn't mean there aren't exceptions. Read these descriptions and see if one jumps out at you as your own style of coping with conflict in the workplace.

What is the accommodating conflict management style?

> When someone has the passive communication style, they are much more likely to be accommodating to the other person involved in the conflict. A passive individual is going to resolve conflict by giving the more aggressive or assertive communicator whatever they are asking for, even if it isn't the best solution for all.
>
> The biggest problem with the accommodating conflict management style is that it allows the other person to

get everything they are asking for, while you could end up with nothing in return. Sometimes being accommodating to quickly resolve a conflict is tempting, and sometimes it really works. If it is an issue that you're not overly invested in, letting the other side "win" can sometimes be in your best interest.

On the other hand, accommodating conflict management styles can be inappropriate if used all the time. Especially if you are in a supervisory or management position, you should be aware that giving in all the time, or even just some of the time, can undermine your own authority and make it more difficult to stand your ground with those employees or coworkers in the future.

What is the avoiding conflict management style?

People who tend to have the passive-aggressive communication style are more likely to use the avoiding conflict management style. This is exactly what it sounds like. Someone who uses avoidance to cope with conflict does not "win" or "lose," they simply refuse to participate. They avoid the conflict, and the individual causing it, at all costs.

Of course, an angry or frustrated person is not likely to allow you to just walk away and ignore the problem. That is why this conflict management style usually results in one of two strategies: either being completely accommodating or forcing the issue through the chain of command.

The problem with this is that eventually you must deal with the situation. It rarely happens that problems go away without being addressed. In fact, avoiding the conflict entirely could just exacerbate it.

You should never ignore conflict in the workplace. Avoiding conflict only allows problems to snowball. If you are a passive-aggressive person you are already more likely to lash out when the passive approach fails or is ignored.

However, avoiding conflict temporarily can be a good thing. Giving yourself and the other party time to cool-off and let tempers ease back to normal levels can reopen the lines of communication. This gives you and the other person a chance to examine the situation from both sides and approach it in a collaborative way with an amicable solution.

What is the compromising conflict management style?

If you are dealing with a manipulative or aggressive communicator, you may need to do some quick thinking and quick talking to keep the situation under control. When you need a fast resolution, compromising can be the best solution. Taking on a compromising conflict management style is easiest for those with an assertive communication style.

The most effective compromises end in a lose-lose situation. Both parties should come away feeling as though they got the short end of the stick. However, both sides should also get some of the things they wanted out of the situation. A master manipulator may seem as though they are willing to compromise, when they truly stack the deck against the other person in the conflict. Be aware of these manipulative communicators so that you are ready to combat them in these situations.

Of course, compromise is not the way to handle all workplace conflict. Sometimes a compromise is impossible. Other times, compromise may not be the most effective method of resolution. When you always compromise to address conflict, you can inadvertently create an environment and culture of resentment.

What is the competing conflict management style?

Aggressive communicators are bound to try and compete during conflict. When someone is an aggressive communicator, they can be completely against compromise or collaboration. They are much more likely to lash out, stand their ground, and do their best to get their way regardless of the feelings, needs, or desires of others.

When supervisors and managers use this conflict resolution style, they often come off as authoritarian and unreasonable. However, sometimes it is necessary. If the conflict is caused by a matter of morals, ethics, or policy, there may be no room for compromise or other tactics. You may have no choice but to stand your ground and cope with the consequences as they arise.

On the other hand, whenever you must compete with someone else to resolve a conflict, it can often end in confrontation, either through heated argument or even violent outbursts. This is because the people that are most likely to have the competing conflict resolution style are also the most aggressive in the workplace. Passive-aggressive individuals are also likely to lash out when faced with a competing conflict management style.

What is the collaboration conflict management style?

This is almost always the best way to handle conflict in the workplace, and as such it shouldn't be a surprise that the collaboration conflict management style is easiest for those with an assertive communication style.

This style goes far beyond simple compromise. Collaboration is an approach in which both parties work together to find a solution. This can be very difficult to instigate with someone who is being passive-aggressive, aggressive, or manipulative. These individuals may outright refuse to participate in collaboration if this solution is presented. On the other hand, you may be able to bring things around to collaboration with some well-thought-out arguments and questions.

In other words, you do not need to be on the same page as the other party to use collaboration to resolve conflict. You can ask probing questions to determine what resolution the other party wants or needs, and to determine how you might be able to answer those needs. You can also make suggestions and ask for the other party's opinion on those suggestions.

By using the collaboration conflict management style in this way, you can make good progress toward a lasting resolution, even if the other party isn't being overly cooperative in the process.

This is about finding a win-win solution rather than the lose-lose of compromise. With collaboration, you work together to find a solution that is good for all. Compromise is more about one side offering the other some caveat in return for what they want, which isn't amicable at all in the end.

When it comes right down to it, everyone should opt for the collaboration conflict resolution method whenever possible. Doing so creates a workplace culture where people feel valued, heard, understood, and appreciated. However, this resolution method can take more time, and time is not something everyone has in every situation.

Even if you use another conflict resolution style as a stop gap, it is best to readdress the issue later after tempers have cooled so that you can revisit the issue with the collaboration method. This way the issue is resolved once and for all, and you will not worry about that conflict again in the future.

How to Determine Your Natural Conversation and Conflict Management Styles

Now that you know what the different conversation and conflict management styles are, you need to learn how to apply these to your own communication and conflict resolution abilities and skills. As you read through the different styles and their definitions, you probably discovered little tidbits that you recognized within yourself. Now is the time to take a more in-depth look at how these styles might apply to you.

If you want to truly understand your natural way of communicating and dealing with conflict, you should take an analytical approach. In addition to self-assessments to categorize your behaviors and speech, you should also ask your coworkers, peers, or even friends and family to give their opinions and assessments as well.

Communication Style Self-Assessment

The easiest way to determine your communication style is by taking a self-assessment. These are readily available online, but don't just do a quick Google search for a quiz. You want to use self-assessments that are grounded in the science of interpersonal communication. For that, you will need to look for assessments available through universities and other workplace experts.

When you go through these self-assessments, make sure that you are being honest with yourself. If you are lying to yourself about how you behave during conversations or conflict, you are not going to be able to improve upon your conflict resolution skills. Identifying our faults is every bit as important as identifying our strengths, in this and everything that we do.

How to Determine Your Communication Style

The best way to get insight into your natural communication style is to talk to the people you interact with every day. Go to your colleagues, or even your friends and family. Ask them these questions to help guide you to learn what communication style you tend towards naturally:

1. Do you maintain eye contact during conversation? If not, where do you look? The floor, the wall behind them, or somewhere else?
2. How do you tend to make decisions? Do you weigh all the options, or jump to the decision that seems best for you in the moment?

3. Do you enjoy small talk, or do you use small talk to open the doors to communication?
4. Do you become frustrated when a conversation gets off-topic?
5. Are you more likely to jump to action or deal with problems in a systematic way?
6. What is your natural posture?
7. How do you tackle personal problems or attacks of conscience?
8. Do you tend to let others make the decisions in the house, such as what to have for dinner or what television shows to watch?
9. Do you often feel resentment even though you don't speak up for yourself?
10. Have you ever found yourself listening to respond so that you can turn the tables of the discussion in your favor?

There are many other things that you could ask yourself to help you determine your communication style. If you want to be certain of your communication style in the workplace, you should talk to your colleagues or managers to get their take on your natural methods of communication. You may be surprised at what they tell you.

In the end, you can use all the information in earlier chapters of this book to determine the communication style of others or yourself. The key here is to be honest with yourself, because until you can recognize your true communication and conflict management styles you will not be able to make the changes necessary to be more effective in resolving conflict in the workplace.

Tips for Consciously Being Assertive and Collaborating

As you can see, the most effective methods of coping with workplace conflict are the assertive communication style combined with the collaborating conflict management style. These two styles go hand in hand to resolve workplace issues in an amicable and calm manner.

Regardless of your natural tendencies for communication or conflict management, it is possible to adapt your communication and conflict management styles to the more effective assertive/collaborating combination. It can take some effort and a bit of practice, but over the course of a few years you will eventually become a natural with these more effective means of communicating and resolving conflict. You must remain vigilant and consciously make decisions about how you will handle a situation to be certain you will cope with them with the appropriate strategies.

One way you can work on discovering how you communicate and make improvements is by keeping a daily journal. Note your general health, mental and emotional state along with any troubling situations and how you handled them. You can go back over these entries later to get a clearer understanding of your behaviors and speech during conflict. Often people read through their own journals in shock as they take on a different perspective over time.

Think of this as a journey of self-discovery and self-improvement that will serve you well, not just at work, but in your personal relationships also. When you can recognize your natural proclivities, the style and skills necessary for reasonable conflict resolution, and discover that they do not coincide, you will be able to make changes that will benefit you in the workplace and beyond.

How to Adjust Your Natural Conversational Style to the Assertive Style

As already mentioned, the assertive communication style is the best for the workplace, especially when it comes to conflict resolution. When you use the assertive communication style, you can take control of the situation while still letting the other party feel as though they are being heard and that their issues are being addressed appropriately.

It takes time to learn how to speak assertively without coming off as abrupt, uncaring, or condescending. You may not get the hang of it right away. You should pay close attention to your speech in the coming weeks or months, catching when you're moving out of the assertive style and consciously making the effort to move back to that position.

Remember that assertive isn't the same as aggressive, and shifting into the aggressive or passive-aggressive communication styles can undermine your efforts. If you find yourself falling out of the assertive style during workplace discussions, use these tips to bring yourself back to the assertive position:

- Make eye contact, even if it seems uncomfortable to do so due to the other person's aggressive, passive-aggressive, or manipulative communication style.
- Stand up straight, but remain relaxed with an open stance. Uncross your arms, and keep them hanging naturally at your sides.

- If you feel yourself getting frustrated and raising your voice, take a deep breath and try again with a calm and modulated tone.
- Timing is everything. If the time doesn't seem to be right, stop the conversation and schedule a more appropriate time to pick it back up.
- Use "I" statements to take power over your feelings and actions while still making the other person responsible for themselves.
- Use calm repetition to shut down manipulative or aggressive communicators and keep yourself under control.
- If you find yourself making assumptions, stop and ask probing questions to ensure you understand the situation without taking away from your own stance.

In truth, you should always strive to use the assertive communication style in all your interactions, both professional and personal. Being assertive means standing up for yourself while still dealing fairly with others. Many people either stand up for themselves aggressively or try too hard to be empathetic, but the best approach is a bit of both worlds.

Developing these traits and skills will also help you be a more effective and assertive communicator in and out of the workplace:

- Learn to be both giving and receiving of respect and understand what that looks like in various situations. Respect is defined as the ability to give something or someone value and treat them with adequate consideration. Being respectful does not mean being a door-mat. It does mean being considerate of the feelings of others even if they do not seem reasonable or align with your own. Find that middle ground and you'll be much more effective in all your interactions with others.

- Be genuine and sincere in all your communications, even if doing so puts you in a bad light. It is much more important to appear human and truly yourself than to make yourself seem perfect. (After all, no one is really perfect.) If you find yourself trying to put a good spin on a bad situation, evaluate whether or not you are giving a fair representation of the circumstances. If it's obvious to you that you're attempting to sell ice to an Eskimo, it's probably even more obvious to the person you're talking to.

- Engender self-confidence, not by being prideful or superior, but by understanding and valuing yourself and others. There is a big difference between having self-confidence and having a big ego. Keep yourself in check by making sure you're not exaggerating your abilities or contributions.

- Develop emotional control by learning to regulate your emotions rather than suppress them. Emotional control isn't something that comes easily to everyone, but it is definitely a must for developing appropriate communication and conflict resolution skills. You cannot remain objective during conflict if you have an emotional response.

- Set boundaries and stick to them. This should apply to all your interpersonal relationships, inside and out of the workplace. Setting and maintaining boundaries is good practice for assertive behavior that can carry over to your communication style with others.

- Be emotionally independent, so that your emotions are not ruled by the actions or speech of the other party. It can be difficult to keep yourself in check, especially when a manipulator is deliberately attempting to evoke an emotional response. When you start feeling yourself get emotional, ask yourself where that emotion is coming from and suppress it if it is really coming from someone else.

As you are working to develop this assertive communication style, keep a record of your progress as well as obstacles that come up along the way.

Chapter 5: Work and Leadership Styles Defined, and How they Clash to Cause Conflict

In addition to understanding the different styles of communication and how to address them, it is also important to ensure that you are creating teams with complimentary work styles. When you create a work environment in which each employee and manager's unique work and leadership styles complement each other, conflict rarely occurs.

But there are a lot of reasons that effort might not happen. When organizations are going through times of change, building effective teams and leadership may not be possible right away. You will need to have leadership that is able to resolve conflicts between people of different backgrounds and talents.

This chapter is divided into two sections, one defining work styles and the other defining leadership styles. Those in management or supervisory positions should consider both their work style and leadership style, how the two might relate, and how the two might clash to create or contribute to workplace conflict.

Conflicting Work styles that can Lead to Inter-employee Conflict

Everyone has their own work style, and most can be divided into the categories we'll touch on below. Even if you are in management, you still have a personal work style for the tasks and responsibilities that you must address each day.

Identifying your own work style can help you make appropriate choices when it comes to career advancements or changes, as well as help you work more closely with others in collaboration. Identifying work styles of others and putting them in appropriate positions is also important for success on both a business and personal career level.

More than this, understanding the work styles of everyone on your team will help you avoid situations that could lead to potential conflict. When you throw two completely opposite work styles together on one project, you are very likely to deal with resulting conflict before the project is completed. Giving the right people the right workload will go a long way toward keeping conflict out of the mix when tensions are high.

What Does the Logical Work Style Look Like?

Who in the office do you go to when you have a difficult math problem, spreadsheet formula, or complex product issues? This is your local logical worker.

The logical work style invariably comes from the analytical mind. These workers can break down complex problems and come to solutions quickly. Logical thinkers are not only likely to agree to neutral talks to resolve conflict, they are also likely to be the forerunners in proposing solutions that work for everyone, creating the most effective win-win situations.

But the logical team member may also be the cause of workplace conflict. Sometimes the most analytical thinkers have a hard time getting creative with resolution. It can be very difficult to convince them when they are wrong, especially if they can't see past their own seemingly logical argument. Persisting in your position can be construed as unreasonable and the person may move from assertive to aggressive quickly.

Other signs someone has the logical work style

Logical people use analytical skills throughout every part of their lives. They are logical thinkers, learners, and workers. As such, you might notice the logical team member immediately during their training, because they will display some obvious traits. These might include:

- Relying on a specific order, chronological steps, or set procedures to complete tasks and work out problems.
- Able to make connections and recognize patterns with ease, especially when it comes to analyzing data, but also when looking at behaviors and social situations.
- Extremely organized, needing everything to have its place, and having a specific way of managing tasks and documents.
- Makes decisions based on the facts of the scenario rather than the emotional responses of themselves and others.
- Strategically attacks problems to systematically find the root of the matter and resolve it to the benefit of all involved, often without being asked to tackle the problem.
- Breaks down problems into multiple task lists and does well when delegating tasks to others.

Logical thinkers are always up to a challenge. Even when conflict doesn't involve logical people, involving them in the conflict resolution process as a third-party mediator is highly encouraged. They are most likely to see both sides of the situation with stark observation to come up with an impartial solution. They are also able to see the situation from a data-driven angle that can strip all the emotion out of a situation to make it easier to resolve.

How to approach someone with the logical work style

If you use the assertive communication style with the collaborative conflict management style as recommended, you should have no issues when approaching someone of a logical mind. Logical thinkers respect people who are straight-forward in explaining what they want and why. They also respect people who approach the situation systematically, rather than emotionally.

People who think analytically are most likely to have either the assertive or aggressive communication style. These individuals are very adamant about logic as they see it. In more humble people, this can create a natural tendency toward communicating with assertion. On the other hand, someone who has often been challenged, or feels their logic is currently being challenged, could be very aggressive in defense of their logic.

When negotiating with such people to resolve conflict, you must be prepared to back up your suggestions for a solution with indisputable facts. Perhaps the best way to think of this approach is to think back to the days of high school or college debate. Prepare factual arguments for any opposition to conflict resolution, and you'll be ready to tackle complex issues collaboratively with any analytically minded person.

What is the Detail-oriented Work Style?

Detail-oriented people often have a hard time seeing the forest for the trees. They can become so hyper-focused on the details that they fail to see the big picture. This can make it difficult for them to see solutions to conflict, because they aren't focused on the overall root cause. Instead, they are focused on all the small conflicts that have arisen as a result of the primary issue at hand.

On the other hand, detail-oriented people can be an asset when collaborating to find solutions. Whereas logical workers have difficulty planning, detail-oriented workers excel in planning but fail in execution. Having a detail-oriented person evaluate plans to mitigate conflict can bring to light errors in the plan that need to be addressed for a long-term solution.

Other signs someone has a detail-oriented work style

It is very easy to spot someone with the detail-oriented work style. Think about the people you work with - who is constantly making lists? Who do you go to for that final edit of an important report? Who do you rely on to find discrepancies in data? These are your detail-oriented workers.

The issue with detail-oriented people is that they may get obsessed with one small piece of a problem, creating far too much conflict over something trivial while taking focus away from more important aspects of the problem or project. While detail-oriented employees are better at avoiding conflict through careful checking of every aspect of a situation, they can also impede the progress of conflict resolution as they hound each tiny detail of the negotiations.

Some other signs that someone is detail-oriented include:

- They triple check their work, and are often anxious until they get explicitly expressed approval.
- They ask a lot of questions, constantly questioning their own recollection and double checking everything.
- They produce high-quality work, but often work right up to deadline making tweaks and edits, rarely completely satisfied before turning in assignments.
- They are the epitome of perfectionism, showing signs of such from the way they dress to the way they keep their workstation.
- They also demand perfection from others, and they get aggressive when they feel someone else's lack of attention to detail causes problems for them or their team.

The issue that some people run into when working with detail-oriented workers is that they don't collaborate well with others on projects. Because they are so invested in the accuracy of their work, they tend to micromanage others when working on group projects. This can also come about when collaborating to resolve conflict. It is far too easy to let a detail-oriented person hijack collaborations and derail conflict resolution efforts. Avoid such by allowing them input, but sidestep using them as advocates for immediate resolution.

How to approach someone with the detail-oriented work style

When approaching someone of the detail-oriented work style in conflict, it is important to remember that they can get hung up on small details, failing to see the objective solutions you are proposing. You must acknowledge their dedication to their work, give them the freedom to express the details that mean the most to them, and then make them see the big picture so that a final solution can be reached.

When you approach a conflict with a detail-oriented person, it is best to make sure they know you recognize their due diligence and efforts. As you lay out suggestions for resolution of the conflict, ask them to work out the minute details of the plan. This gives them the ability to lend their expertise to the collaboration, without letting talks get derailed by tiny issues that distract everyone from the meat of the issue.

What is the Supportive Work Style?

It is perhaps the easiest to recognize the supportive work style, because these employees are the most helpful. Who do you go to when you have a task that you just don't have time to complete? Who in the office seems to enjoy the tedious, minute tasks that no one else likes to do? Which teammate do you go to when you need help brainstorming an idea or problem? These are your supporters.

Supportive people are there to make everyone's life easier. They are often very good at the mundane tasks and paperwork that others dislike, and they don't mind taking those tasks on in favor of getting rid of more complex tasks or problems. The supportive workers are usually those that stay in mid-level positions throughout their career, simply because they feel more comfortable supporting others than standing up for themselves.

Of course, that means when it comes to conflict resolution, these workers are much more likely to be passive and accommodating. They aren't likely to rock the boat, even if they feel others are taking advantage of them. Supportive people work hard to appear as such, and they don't want to mar that reputation by being forceful or aggressive.

On the other hand, like other passive communicators, supportive people do have their breaking point, and tempers can flare seemingly out of nowhere. It is important to always be observant of body language and other subtle clues that someone who is working hard to appear submissive on the surface is really about to blow their temper, making a conflicting situation harder to resolve.

Other signs someone has the supportive work style

There are a lot of people out there that try to be supportive at work because they feel it will help their careers in the long run. How do you know you are working with one of them, or someone that has the supportive work style naturally? Here are some additional signs someone is more supportive in the workplace:

- They tend to be much more emotionally expressive, including dramatic changes in tone, speed, and volume of speech, as well as facial expressions.
- Supportive workers talk with their hands to show excitement and eagerness.
- They will show empathy more often than any other emotion when discussing issues with colleagues or customers.

- Supportive workers get excited and show a dramatic display of enthusiasm when you approach them with new projects or responsibilities.
- Supportive workers love to take the initiative to solve problems before they become significant pain points.
- Many supportive workers are very organized and detail oriented.

Most conflict with supportive workers stems from their tendency to take on everything asked of them or delegated to them, without any consideration for their own needs or schedules. You might have guessed by now that supportive workers are often passive communicators. They tend to allow themselves to be doormats, taking on whatever is handed to them until they reach a breaking point.

When the workload and/or stress finally become too much, the explosive reaction can seem to come out of nowhere. In addition, tasks and deadlines that were promised by the supportive worker can end up getting dropped altogether if their juggling act falls apart, and that alone can create conflict in the chaos that ensues. Supportive workers in a non-supportive environment are likely to become passive-aggressive in both communication and actions.

How to approach someone with the supportive work style

The good news is that supportive workers thrive on collaboration, so finding yourself in conflict with such individuals isn't usually difficult to manage. While the assertive communication style with the collaborating conflict management style is ideal when dealing with any conflict, supportive workers will be the most receptive to such an approach.

If you have a problem with a supportive worker, and they are being pleasant and passive as usual, you can usually approach them with a simple, straight-forward assertive style with an offer of collaborating to find a solution. Remember to have some possible solutions ready to throw out on the table so that they know you mean business and are more receptive to the process.

On the other hand, if a supportive worker has suddenly become overwhelmed to the point of tasks not being completed and deadlines being missed, it may be necessary to take a slightly different approach. While it is still important to be assertive and make collaborative efforts to resolve the conflict, it is just as important to show empathy and understanding. Supportive workers don't want to be in conflict with others, so if you can show them that you understand how they got to this point and that you are ready to help them fix it, you will get far in resolving the issue quickly.

It is also important to note that if you want to permanently prevent future conflict with a supportive worker, you should collaborate with them to find solutions that keep them from being overwhelmed with work in the future. Each work situation can be vastly different, but the idea is to take stress from this person so that they can perform duties efficiently and accurately, and without causing conflict.

How Does the Idea-oriented Person Work?

Idea-oriented workers are always thinking of the big picture. They are amazing problem solvers because they easily find opportunities where others only see complications or improbabilities. When an obstacle comes up in the path, the convergent thinker is the one that will find a way to blast it out of the way of progress.

Fortunately, that means that they make a great ally in collaborating to find solutions to conflicting situations. While you should always have some idea of how you would like to solve the root issues at hand, these individuals are often best at finding the solutions that create a win for everyone. In addition to being well-behaved in workplace conflicts in which they find themselves, idea-oriented people are great mediators in resolving the conflict of others.

Other signs someone has the idea-oriented work style

> It's always easy to pinpoint the grandiose thinkers within your team or organization. These individuals love to throw out ideas from the top of their heads. They seem to always be thinking about different opportunities, and they like to inspire others to take advantage of them. But big thinkers often fail to consider the little details.

> These people are always thinking outside the box, and as such they are great to have around when resolving conflict, even if you have them on board as an unbiased mediator. They are also great at spotting opportunities, so some great progress can be made in a project or department completely separate from resolving the conflict at hand.

> Some common signs you are working with an idea-oriented person are:

- They get very excited about their ideas and visions of opportunity and work hard to inspire others to believe in the same.
- These workers enjoy having their ideas challenged so that they can find obstacles and revise their visions, creating genius overall plans that may or may not work depending on actual resources.
- Because they think big and ignore details, the ideas that these individuals have aren't always feasible.
- They tend to interject big ideas with little or no forethought.
- They can get defensive and shut down if required to flesh out the details of their monumental proposals.

In addition to coming up with general ideas that are typically very innovative, these individuals are also great at helping others find the solutions to their work-related issues. They can break down problems quickly and come up with ideas that others wouldn't think of, but that work out to be the best solution possible. On the other hand, they aren't going to help you figure out how to make it happen.

How to approach someone with the idea-oriented work style

People with the idea-oriented work style are most likely to be assertive communicators. This means they may not be quite as approachable as other employees. On the other hand, they are likely to be very explicit about what they need, as well as what they expect from their team and colleagues.

Depending on personalities or previous personal history, assertive communication can deteriorate to aggressive communication, and sometimes rather quickly. For that reason, it is a good idea to address conflict with a neutral third party available to help keep things civil and moving forward.

Other than that, resolving conflict with such individuals is rather simple. Because big-picture thinkers are also great at seeing problems or obstacles from all sides, they make great collaborators, especially with other assertive detail-oriented people. If you and the person with whom you are trying to resolve conflict are both big-idea thinkers, you might consider getting a detail-oriented person to play moderator.

Just make sure that you remain open during your negotiations with idea-centered people. While you might still go into the situation with possible resolutions in mind, you should be prepared to change your views or plans to incorporate other avenues or considerations that these workers will undoubtedly contribute to the discussions.

Conflicting Leadership Styles that can Lead to Dissention

For many, resolving conflict within teams or departments is not a great feat. But those same individuals can struggle when trying to resolve conflict with colleagues across divisions, especially if you have conflicting leadership styles.

Anytime you are resolving conflict with people that are on the same organizational level that you are, your leadership style will come into play. This is because when everyone involved is typically the leader of their group, they find it difficult to follow or collaborate.

As a manager or supervisor, you have a leadership style that you bring to your team that will be different than the styles of other team leaders. When team leaders must collaborate, or if there are disputes between employees of both teams, it can cause feelings of defensiveness and dissension before a productive conversation can ever begin.

Before you approach conflict with other leaders, consider your own leadership style and the style of the individual or individuals with whom you are trying to resolve conflict. If those leadership styles are conflicting in any way, make sure to incorporate those considerations into your conflict resolution strategy.

What is the Autocratic or Authoritative Leadership Style?

The autocratic leadership style, also considered an authoritative approach, is based on ruling with an iron fist. These leaders like to be the ones in charge. They don't like to share decision making or planning activities, and they rarely ask for input from their team or others outside their departments. These leaders are the hardest to collaborate with because they are so used to being in charge, and don't want to give even an inch in negotiations.

On the other hand, an autocratic leader is someone who is extremely decisive, which can make them great problem solvers. If you can get them into a collaborating mood, or if you can get a mediator to ask the right probing questions to determine the root issues at hand, they can be a great asset in coming up with executable and effective solutions.

81

Take a moment to consider the other leaders in your organization. Who do you think of when you need a prompt decision or swift action? Who always tries to take control of the meeting? Who is the most stubborn? These are your authoritative leaders.

Authoritative leaders like to think they are in charge, even when they are not. They can sometimes be forceful in trying to achieve a common goal. Most authoritative leaders are aggressive communicators as well. Other employees in the workplace may feel intimidated by their grandiose notions and unrealistic expectations.

There are a few other definite signs that you are dealing with an authoritative leader.

- They create highly structured environments with lots of processes and procedures in place to have the most control over how teams complete their work.
- They discourage out-of-the-box thinking in favor of tried-and-true principles and standards.
- These leaders like everything to be outlined in detail, and procedures clearly communicated, with training programs that seem to go "overboard."
- They probably expect to be the ones to choose where the team goes for lunch, and likely get upset when their choice is vetoed by the rest of the group.
- They don't like to be told they are wrong, or that they can't have something they have decided they need.

It can be very difficult to work with an autocratic leader, especially if you are trying to do so by meeting them on the same level. If you are a subordinate, the idea of striking up a difficult conversation with an authoritative supervisor can be terrifying. If the leader is your own subordinate, you may have difficulty getting them to take direction if they don't agree with your methods.

How to approach an autocratic leader with a problem

How you approach an autocratic leader depends on what capacity you are trying to resolve the conflict. If you are on the same organizational level as the authoritative leader, you must first make it clear that you are not their subordinate, and that you require the same respect and consideration that they themselves expect in return. From there, it can be easier to work together to find solutions, but these individuals will still be hard to negotiate with.

If you are the subordinate of an autocratic leader and you are having a conflict with that person, you should not try to handle the matter on your own. Go to the next level of management or your human resources department, whichever is dictated by your organization's structure and policies. These people can exert authority over your own team leader, which will go a long way toward resolving the root problem between you and the offending autocratic supervisor.

Of course, if you yourself are that individual's supervisor, it should not be difficult for you to take control of the conflicting situation. The fact is that because these leaders believe in the iron will of authority, they in turn respect authority as it applies to themselves. That can make your job a lot easier, especially if you can then get them involved in collaborating for solutions.

What is the Pacesetting Style of Leadership?

By all rights, all managers and business leaders should adopt a pacesetting attitude. Pacesetters are those individuals that like to set the stage for their team's success. Their goal is to keep progress driving forward, while the team continually strives for improvements in efficiency and performance. While this is a great way to break records, beat deadlines, and increase sales or service, it is also completely unsustainable on its own.

On the other hand, when you go about leadership with a pacesetting attitude in addition to using parts of other leadership styles, you will be able to move your team forward at a reasonable pace while still making industry improvements and progress on projects that stimulate growth in the organization, and the industry as a whole.

Unfortunately, there are always those who go to extremes. If you are dealing with a pacesetting leader that doesn't take on other roles within the team or across departments, you are likely going to run into some issues when it comes to resolving conflict. For one thing, pacesetters always think that new ideas are better than old ones, and that means you will have a hard time resolving situations that require new and innovative solutions.

Other signs you are dealing with a pace-setter

Pacesetters are another type of businessperson that is easy to spot in the workplace. Which team leader sets the highest standards for their team? What colleague is always trying to push for new procedures or policies when they don't seem to be warranted? Who is always coming to you with an article from an industry publication with admonitions to "jump on the bandwagon" of trending business activities or projects? These are your pacesetters.

Some other indications that you are dealing with a pacesetter include:

- They are obsessive when it comes to speed and efficiency of work processes and structures.
- They often assume that people know what is expected of them on the job, and they don't like to try to coach people or train them.
- They also don't like to give people training or instruction more than once, and they can become irate when you ask them to explain something they feel you should already know or understand.
- These individuals are very task oriented, and they expect everyone else to be as well.
- They will often check in with others to make sure their work is being done quickly and accurately, and will expect to visually see progress in their task management.

When you are resolving conflict with a pacesetter, they are likely to try to find all types of excuses for why the issue occurred in the first place. Once you get them to pin down the actual problem, you can work toward finding solutions. The problem with the pacesetter is that they are likely to shoot down most of the solutions you present, because they want a new solution that may not be within current organizational policies.

How to approach a pace-setter

Pacesetters aren't going to want the same old solutions to work-related problems. They want new solutions so that they can feel they have made a difference in the way the organization functions. They may not want to take responsibility for their part in the conflict, and you will need to convince them of this before you will be able to get them to work on a solution.

When it comes to finding solutions, they will do their best to try to get you to change company policy or procedures to meet their ideas for an equitable solution. If you present solutions that they have heard or tried before, they probably aren't going to want to consider them again. If it is possible to have some flexibility, consider giving them a bit of space so that they can come to a more collaborating attitude. If not, you'll need to be assertive, firm about your position, and clear in why their demands are not acceptable.

Approach pacesetters with the idea in mind that they like to be innovative and trendy. If you can present a conflict resolution strategy that incorporates their drive for progress and the structural processes of your organization, you will have a much easier time working with them on a long-term solution.

It is important not to let these leaders control the conversation and lead it away from solutions and into the realm of contemplation and probabilities. Pacesetters are always thinking of a problem from all angles, which can be helpful, but it can also create chaos. It is best for everyone to have something of a pacesetting attitude in the business world, but it has no place in conflict resolution.

What is the Democratic Leadership Style?

The democratic leadership style is just what it sounds like. Someone who leads democratically often seeks the input and approval of all involved or impacted by a decision. They want to make sure that everyone gets what they need, and they are amazing at coming up with win-win-win solutions to common workplace conflicts. In short, democratic leaders know they are in charge, but they also know that often the best way to manage a team is by giving everyone a voice.

Of course, it isn't possible to rule democratically all the time, and that's why these individuals don't always find their footing right away when they are projected into leadership roles. But democratic leaders are easier to work with when you are approaching them as a colleague on their level, especially if they respect you and your position.

The problem with democratic leaders is that in their pursuit to be fair, they often overcomplicate things and try to enforce complex agreements that are hardly necessary. In looking at a conflict from all angles and trying to give everyone involved and impacted a voice, they can also spend so much time in deliberation that no action ever gets taken.

When dealing with democratic leaders as equals to resolve a conflict, you must be ready to keep them on the same page as everyone else. They tend to get lost in their thoughts as they consider every nuance of the problem at hand. You may also notice that these leaders, when put in collaboration with other leaders, tend to fall to the sidelines until they feel they must speak up in the name of fairness or justice.

Other signs you are dealing with a democratic leader

The democratic leader is the one that likes to hold a lot of team meetings, both as a group and on an individual basis. They want to make sure that everyone is on the same page, and that everyone can give their input, but the two mix as well as oil and water. The more voices in the pool of possible solutions, the easier it is for communication to break down, and confusion and chaos will follow.

In general, democratic leaders are very open-minded and unprejudiced individuals that are easy to get along with as long as you are treating them (and everyone else) fairly. They are usually more than willing to participate in collaboration to find solutions to conflict, whether within their own teams or across departments.

Some other signs that you are working with a democratic personality include:

- They urge people to think outside the box, voice their thoughts and opinions, and collaborate for the best solution.
- They rarely decide on their own without consulting at least one other person, usually someone directly related to the situation being dealt with in that moment.
- They are more likely to recognize others for their accomplishments and contributions to the team and the organization.

- Democratic leaders love to motivate their team with fun games, competitions, and incentives, which are usually highly effective.

Democratic leaders usually use the assertive communication style, and they are very good collaborators when it comes to resolving conflict. They are great to have as part of a mediation as well because they will work hard to make each side see from the other point of view. Sometimes this is all that is necessary for people to be able to put aside their differences and resolve an issue once and for all so that they can work together successfully in the future.

How to approach a democratic leader

The democratic-minded person is perhaps the easiest to approach with the need to resolve a conflict or problem situation. They always want to hear everyone's side of a situation, understand, and offer empathy, and are constantly driven to find equitable solutions that are win-win-win for all involved. That means they are ready to solve the problem before you ever present it to them.

However, it is still important not to let the democratic thinker get ahead of themselves. In trying to see a situation from all sides and find the most honorable solution, they may get lost in details that don't matter in the grand scheme of things. Let these individuals lead the collaboration to resolve conflict, but keep them in check and on target.

What is the Coaching Style of Leadership?

When someone adopts the coaching style of leadership, they are usually focusing their efforts on increased team performance through careful training, skill building, and other support to help all employees in their purview to be as successful as possible, not just in their current position but throughout their careers.

Coaches usually measure their own success by the success of their teams, as well as how their overall team's performance and their own contributions correlate to the success of the entire company. As such, they are always looking for conflict resolutions that are best from a business-minded standpoint.

This can be an advantage in some situations, where clear analytical thought and careful planning are required for long-term resolution. On the other hand, this staunch "bottom line" thinking can cause them to think of team members only as a human resource, thus neglecting the more human needs of their workers.

Other signs someone uses the coaching leadership style

"What's up, coach?" Remember that confident, rigid posture your physical education teachers had in primary school? The leaders in your company that adopt a coaching style will remind you very much of these people. These individuals are always ready to help someone succeed, and they are definitely in the mind of being problem solvers.

Here are some other traits of those who prefer the coaching leadership style:

- Coaches make sure their team knows that they have the final say, even as they ask for their input as to what will help them improve their performance and be more successful, both now and in the future.
- They tend to want to work together to resolve conflict and find solutions to routine workplace issues in a collaborative effort, but they may not interject a lot if there are multiple people involved in the discussion.
- Individuals used to coaching others are going to be less likely to want to take coaching themselves.
- These leaders enjoy collaborating with their peers to resolve complex issues, but they aren't likely to put forth any original ideas for solutions on their own.

In short, those who approach the coaching style of leadership are always the easiest to collaborate with in conflict resolution. It is generally argued that most managers and workplace leaders should incorporate the coaching style at least to some extent. Like the assertive communication style and the collaborative conflict resolution strategy, the coaching style correlates to productive and equitable conflict resolution. This also makes them very good to have as mediators.

How to approach someone who likes to coach subordinates

The only problem you may have when approaching a coach with a conflict is if they do not see you as an equal or superior. If you are their direct peer, you can usually approach them with a collaborative spirit and make swift progress toward a resolution, long before the conflict becomes explosive. If your position is above theirs in your company's structure, you will be

91

able to get their help resolving the conflict quickly if you just let them know that their expertise is needed. This is enough to get their ego going and get them involved in conflict resolution.

Once you have the coach at your negotiating table, conflict resolution is easy to manage with these individuals. From here, it is a simple matter to encourage their collaborative nature, which may even offer up solutions that you did not think of previously.

What is the Affiliative Style of Leadership?

Affiliative leaders are those who are the most empathetic toward the individuals within their teams and organization. Those who adopt the affiliative leadership style are more concerned with meeting the emotional and social needs of their team members and how it relates to their overall success than they are with performance metrics.

This can be both good and bad. On one hand, businesspeople that take the thoughts and feelings of others into consideration are more likely to resolve conflicts in a way that is fair for all involved. On the other hand, when too much emphasis is placed on the emotions of those involved in a conflict, it can take away from the goal of the team or organization.

While it is important for all managers and business leaders to show empathy in the workplace, as well as work to meet the emotional social needs of teams and colleagues as truly required, it is vital that these do not become the goal of conflict resolution. Rather, meeting the emotional and social needs of those involved should be considered a means to conflict resolution, not the end goal or result.

People who take on the affiliative leadership style are those that you might think of as push-overs. When their subordinates approach them with an emotional plea or excuse for, say, an attendance violation, these leaders are likely to let the discrepancies slide. While this can make for happy employees, it can also create very ineffective teams.

Some other signs that you are dealing with someone more in tune to people's emotional needs are:

- They pride themselves on the ability to improve communication, because they strive to always be inclusive and open-minded.
- Their ability to recognize the emotional and social needs of their team members allows them to place people in those positions in which they will excel the most.
- These individuals are easy to trust, and their ability to engender trust between two conflicting sides makes them an asset in mediation attempts.
- Affiliative leaders are usually the most flexible.

As you can see, it can be helpful to have an affiliative person on your side, but when leaders focus too much on emotional and social constructs it can prevent progress. When you are resolving conflict with such a person, they are likely to try to bring the conversation to an emotional level rather than trying to find solutions.

These leaders are also very emotional beings themselves, and that can make for some strange or sudden outbursts. When immersed in conflict, these leaders will be the first to tear up, raise their voice in frustration, or otherwise exhibit grandiose displays of emotion.

How to approach someone who uses the affiliative leadership style

If you need to approach an affiliative leader with a conflict, you should do so from an emotional standpoint. Starting out with that approach will create an instant bond of trust and understanding that will be highly beneficial as you encourage collaboration for a resolution.

The important thing you must remember when dealing with such individuals is that they are likely to come back again and again to the emotions involved, the social needs that should be met in the situation, and what led to the situation in the first place. Such discussions can be helpful in identifying the root cause of a conflict, but they can be very hindering when trying to come up with solutions. You must keep a tight rein on the direction of the conversation.

Chapter 6: How to Recognize and Prevent Conflict

The best way to cope with conflict in the workplace is to head it off before it becomes a real issue. When you can immediately recognize conflict, you will have a better chance of preventing it in the first place. Often, troubling situations in the workplace are born from misunderstandings or limited perspectives, and open communication can resolve the issue before it gets out of hand.

You should always be on the lookout for possible conflict in the workplace. Such conflicts are rarely sudden, even though they may seem so. In reality, most issues between coworkers or colleagues begin long before they are ever mentioned. By the time an inexperienced manager notices the conflict, the problem has already become too large to handle easily.

By being ever vigilant, you will be able to notice the subtle signs of arising conflict and head it off before it becomes a workplace safety issue.

How to Recognize Approaching Conflict

Being able to recognize approaching conflict is one of the most important skills to develop, especially if you plan on advancing your career into the various levels of management. While not all conflict looks the same, there are some definite signs that conflict is about to take place. If your organization is wise, there should be several supervisors in each department to ensure that all employees are receiving adequate attention. This allows signs to be noticed more frequently.

Body Language

Body language is the most important thing to pay attention to when you are talking to someone, especially if you are in a situation that could easily turn sour. Even when a person tries to maintain their composure, body language will show when they are frustrated, angry, or argumentative. Some of the most common body language related to pending conflict is:

- Avoiding eye contact, especially if they normally do not do so. Remember that passive and sometimes passive-aggressive individuals will naturally look elsewhere, so you must take everything into consideration when looking at eye contact and movement.
- Crossed arms are a sign of closing oneself off from the situation. When someone crosses their arms, it is a good indicator that they are not really listening. They may be listening to respond, but they are not getting the meat of what you are trying to convey. Crossed arms also show that someone is unwilling to compromise and is likely to cause a scene if challenged.
- Frowning might seem like an obvious sign of discontent, but how often do you really see people frown? Most of the time frowners are more frustrated and agitated than they are upset or emotional, so this can be an important warning sign.
- Physically distancing themselves or turning away from the speaker.

If you notice any of the above, you should seek out the people involved and attempt to resolve the issue before it escalates. Depending on the individuals, their positions, and the nature of the conflict, you may want to meet with each person individually to get a more complete picture of the problem. When you meet with all parties in the conflict at one time you can discuss the different points of view and come to an equitable resolution.

Behavioral Changes

When it comes to recognizing approaching conflict, you will have much more success with people that you already interact with daily. If you are unfamiliar with someone's normal behavior, it is easy to miss signs that they are about to launch workplace conflict. However, if you work with someone on a daily or weekly basis, you should have a baseline to recognize behavioral changes. These might include:

- Withdrawing from the situation when it would be totally out of character to do so.
- Refusing to contribute to discussion or coming up with solutions to presented problems.
- Blatant attempts at sabotage, while still attempting to maintain an air of innocence.
- Throwing up obstacles to project success to make things more difficult for other team members.
- Remaining quiet and reserved when that is not their natural state. (This is a big clue when it comes to people who tend to be passive or passive-aggressive.)

You may also notice that they become fidgety or otherwise restless, as though they cannot contain their frustration or anger. If you see any signs of someone about to lose their

97

temper, and you fear they may act out their aggression physically, you should make sure that there is at least one other manager available to witness the altercation. If your organization has their own security detail, you may want to notify them so that they can be prepared to deal with any impending situation.

Slowed Productivity

When people are unhappy with a situation, they aren't likely to be very productive. Even if they try to follow through with expected job duties and workplace situations, a lack of focus will dominate their activities. Anytime you notice someone on your team or under your supervision suddenly decreasing their job performance, it is a good indication that conflict is already in the air and brewing.

Signs of Anxiety

People who are afraid of conflict will have very high anxiety when it is about to occur. Even if they are going to be the ones instigating the confrontation due to their own built-up anger, they will have extreme anxiety about doing so. Often the more anxious someone is about addressing a problem the more likely they are to lash out and end in an explosive confrontation.

Constant Complaints

If you notice that someone who is normally easy going starts complaining about everything, it is a good indication that they are very unhappy. They may not even be unhappy about the things that they are complaining about. Instead, they might be frustrated over something completely unrelated. Passive-aggressive individuals are more prone to this.

Showing a Lack of Trust

If you have a coworker or subordinate that suddenly stops trusting you, it could be a sign that they have a bigger beef that needs to be addressed.

Dysfunctional Meetings or Teams

When a team that once worked like clockwork has their progress halted, it is a sign that there is conflict brewing within the group. When meetings or teams are no longer effective at moving forward with projects or performance, it usually means that frustrations and tempers are flaring. People tend to shut down when they are angry, especially if they are of the passive or passive-aggressive persuasion.

Communicating Inappropriately

Perhaps the most obvious clue that conflict is about to launch is a change in appropriate communication. When someone who is normally very communicative shuts down, it is a sign that conflict is afoot within a group or team.

But inappropriate communication can also be a sign of inevitable and immediately pending conflict or confrontation. If an employee or coworker suddenly starts cursing or otherwise using unprofessional language, raises their voice, or speaks in a very aggressive and accusatory tone, you need to immediately take steps to identify the root issue and address it.

How to Approach Different Communication Styles to Prevent Conflict

As we have already discussed, people with different communication styles react to situations in different ways. It is very important that you approach people with the appropriate method and techniques based on their communication style. This helps avoid misunderstandings, and it can help you resolve the issue before true conflict or confrontation occur.

Addressing Issues with Passive Communicators

If you are working with a passive communication style, you're going to do most of the work of conflict prevention and resolution. The first thing you must do is determine what the actual problem is. Passive communicators aren't likely to tell you what that is clearly or voluntarily, so you're going to have to ask probing questions to get to the root of the problem.

It is important to get the individual to tell you what is wrong so that it can be addressed in an appropriate fashion, but it is also important not to push too hard. If the conflict isn't likely to lead to immediate or violent confrontation, it may be a good idea to allow this process to be stretched out over several individual conversations so that the passive person doesn't feel as though they are being bombarded with questions. This feeling of bombardment could be a catalyst for conflict rather than resolving it.

A passive person is used to having their contributions ignored, so when you try to understand their value and what they need to continue to be an asset to the organization, it goes a long way toward putting out that smoldering fuse.

Addressing Issues with Passive-Aggressive
Communicators

Before deciding how to approach a passive-aggressive communicator, you first must determine if they are naturally so or if they are only being passive-aggressive in this instance. If the person you are dealing with is not normally passive-aggressive, taking on this communication style is a clear sign of unhappiness with their position, management, or the company itself.

However, generally many people are passive-aggressive to a fault. Unfortunately, many of these people have fallen naturally into a passive-aggressive communication style due to personal situations that make them question their usual self-confidence, or that has shaken their faith in their ability to make positive change without being a doormat. At the same time, they still have their pride and know their worth, so they are more likely to stand up and fight when pushed.

If you want to address issues with someone who is passive-aggressive, you're going to need to draw them out so that they answer your questions honestly. The passive-aggressive communicator is going to do everything they can to make it seem as though you are getting your way, all the while doing what they can to sabotage the conflict resolution process.

The best approach is to be straightforward and direct. Take on the same strategy as you would for passive individuals, such as asking probing questions and rephrasing for understanding. These can sometimes help the person see that you are trying to discover the problem and find a resolution. If they feel you are on their side, they may drop the more aggressive tendencies and work on collaborating for a resolution, no confrontation required.

Addressing Issues with Manipulative Communicators

Dealing with a manipulative person is difficult in the best of situations, but in the workplace it can be even more difficult to navigate. When someone is intentionally manipulative, they are going to do everything they can to get their way. They will provoke your temper, play with your emotions, or question your intelligence in subtle or blatant ways.

The only way to deal with a manipulative communicator is to remain completely open and honest in your dealings. When you are completely calm and in control of yourself and the situation, the manipulator will not be able to get you to do anything that you don't want to. While this seems like a no-brainer, it can be difficult to implement in the workplace while still maintaining respect and professionalism.

If you feel that someone is trying to manipulate you while you are trying to prevent conflict, call them out on the behavior. Make sure they know that you are well-aware of the actual situation and what came about to cause the conflict. If you aren't certain about the details, now is the time to ask probing questions and employ active listening to determine what needs to be done to resolve the conflict.

Usually when manipulative people are called out on their behavior, they will either become very angry or they will become very agreeable. It could go either way and depends on the individual. If you are going to be dealing with a manipulative person, make sure that you do not do so alone. Have a colleague or human resources professional in the meeting with you to ensure that any confrontational outbursts are dealt with appropriately.

Addressing Issues with Aggressive Communicators

If you are working with an aggressive communicator, you are going to need to tread lightly in how you deal with them if you want to avoid a loud or violent outburst. The most important thing to remember here is that you should NEVER approach an aggressive communicator on your own, especially if you are addressing conflict or a difficult workplace situation.

Aggressive communicators don't often become physically violent in the workplace, but that doesn't mean they aren't a threat to the well-being of others. Showing aggression in any way shouldn't be tolerated. Remember that emotional or mental abuse is still abuse, even if it doesn't leave scars. This isn't just true in relationships, it is also true in the workplace.

Some of the other ways an aggressive coworker might act out include:

- Yelling, screaming, or cursing. This is especially an issue if the individual is within earshot of important customers, clients, leads, or stakeholders.
- Banging on desks, slamming desk drawers, slamming conference room doors etc.
- Making threats, veiled, implied, or blatant, even if those threats are emotional or career-damaging in nature rather than physical.
- Coercive behavior in which they try to take control of the situation and make unreasonable demands.

When dealing with aggressive people in the workplace, it can be tempting to take an accommodating stance to protect yourself and others in the office building. But this is the worst mistake you can make. You must maintain your assertive communication style, remaining clear in your expectations. If you allow an aggressive person to take control of the situation, it will deteriorate quickly as soon as someone disagrees.

Instead, you should deal with aggressive people using the following tools:

- Ally yourself with other colleagues or management staff and present a united front when addressing conflict with aggressive individuals.

- Put yourself in their shoes so that you understand why they are being aggressive. Often understanding the *why* puts you in a better position to address the root issue.

- Keep control of the conversation. They will try to control it, but you must remain on topic and address the issue at hand rather than be distracted by outbursts.

- Maintain your assertiveness and stand up for yourself. Set clear boundaries and maintain your personal space.

- Bring their behavior out into the open in a passive-aggressive way, by saying something like, "I feel there is a hostile air to the room, how do you feel?" This makes them aware that you know they are trying to intimidate you, and it isn't going to work. It is a way of challenging the aggressive behavior without really calling them out on it and provoking their temper.

Aggressive people thrive on conflict, and they try to create it wherever possible, even if it is on a subconscious level. The aggression isn't often hidden, but can be seen by anyone given the opportunity to observe the individual interacting with others in the workplace. Identify your aggressors early, and keep a close eye on them so that you can resolve conflict before it takes hold.

Tools for Avoiding Conflict

When difficult situations arise in the workplace, it can be a simple matter to avoid true conflict or confrontation. In fact, these tools can be used to address any workplace situation in a calm and amicable fashion.

Stay Calm

Your attitude or emotions as you begin a difficult conversation set the tone for the entire interaction. The ability to stay calm in the eye of the storm is a talent that not everyone possesses, but it is a very good trait to develop.

If you can remain calm while others are ranting, yelling, complaining, or being accusatory, you will be much more likely to maintain control of the situation. When you allow yourself to become as upset as the people involved in the conflict, you will not be able to head it off effectively. Instead, you yourself will be contributing to the conflict.

If you have difficulty keeping calm when tempers are flaring, there are a few things you can do to trick your mind into calming down. Often the mind reflects the body, so if you can control breathing and other factors it will slow down your thoughts and help you cool off more quickly. Some of these tricks include:

- Ask for a moment to gather your thoughts, and take five deep, slow breaths in succession, letting each exhale take away your anger and frustration. This only takes a few seconds, but it can save you hours of conflict resolution later.
- Conflict is often further fueled by anxiety, either due to confrontation in general or the possible outcomes of the situation at hand. Ground yourself quickly to reduce anxiety and better open the lines of communication by looking around the room for something you can touch, smell, hear, and taste, and one thing in the room you consider beautiful.

- Maintain an even voice. If you catch your voice rising, make the effort to bring it back down. It will help keep you grounded and in control of your emotions.
- Be prepared to walk away with the conflict unresolved, to be addressed later, either to allow tempers to cool or to gather more information.

Although the cause of the initial conflict may have nothing to do with your own actions, you must recognize your role in conflict resolution. It is vital that you maintain your own equilibrium and tight emotional control if you are to resolve the matter without escalation.

Clearly State Expectations for the Interaction

Before you dive into the root of a problem, make sure that the other party knows what you expect to resolve during the interaction. Set expectations as to attitude and tone, as well as cooperation in resolving the issue at hand. Be prepared to hear their side as well, and make sure that they know this is an option.

Active Listening

Active listening has already been mentioned quite a bit, and for good reason. Active listening skills are extremely important for avoiding conflict. People are much quicker to anger and aggression when they feel that they are not being heard or understood. When you employ active listening skills, you are better able to address the situation at hand as well. To employ active listening, make sure you:

- Focus on the speaker by looking at them directly and listening for understanding rather than response.

- Show that you are listening by using body language, such as turning toward the speaker or maintaining an open posture.

- Provide feedback about what you have been told. If you aren't sure you understand, or if it is very important to the speaker that they are understood, ask probing questions to ensure understanding.

- Don't judge the speaker or the situation before they are finished, and reserve judgment until you have all of the information. Even if the situation calls upon you to make a judgment of some kind, you should do so only after all the information is presented.

Basically, you need to make sure that you are really listening and understanding the other person, because if you are not the situation is not likely to de-escalate.

Don't Make Assumptions

You should never assume what someone else is going to think, feel, or do. Even if you consider yourself somewhat of an empath (many people do), you should still verbally confirm their perspective in their own words. Making assumptions or jumping to conclusions is the biggest contributor to workplace conflict, and it can push an already difficult situation out of control.

Even when one is trying hard to be inclusive, it is still likely that the average person will make certain assumptions based on stereotypes or their own experiences. It is very important that you leave such assumptions behind when resolving conflict. If you do not remain completely inclusive, you will risk escalating the situation further.

Maintaining Positivity

You don't want to be bubbly and outwardly positive when you are dealing with difficult workplace situations. It would be completely out of place. But you don't want to take a pessimistic view of the situation either. It is important to remain positive and optimistic, regardless of the other party's behavior. Continue to point out the good in the situation until the conflict is defused.

Be Tactful in Stating Your Case

When you are in conflict with someone else, especially if you are acting in a supervisory or managerial capacity, it is of the utmost importance that you state your case with tact. In many workplace situations, there is only one possible solution based on company policy or other regulating factors. When that is the case, you must be able to state your position in such a way that they do not take the solution personally.

The biggest thing to remember here is that you cannot respond emotionally. You must leave emotion out of the equation, and address the obvious solution to the conflict with clear expectations. In other words, when your position can't be changed for whatever reason, you need to explain it matter-of-factly so that they understand this is not your choice based on your thoughts or emotions, but rather the best resolution of the conflict for all in the situation.

Attack the Problem, Not the Person

As you get more and more frustrated in dealing with someone trying to cause conflict, it can be tempting to make personal attacks. This is something you should never do in any situation in the workplace. You should never get on a personal level when it comes to workplace conflict, as this is only going to breed directed anger that could lead to very violent outbursts.

Instead, if you find yourself needing to point out the flaws in a situation or action, attack the problem rather than the person. Make sure that you are both focused on what the real problem is, rather than the imagined problem of the other individual.

As a part of this, you should make sure that you avoid the "blame game." The blame game happens when two people involved in a conflict go back and forth about who caused the problem in the first place. Unfortunately, no one wins when these tactics are employed. Blaming each other only fosters more anger and frustration.

Leave the Past Behind and Focus on the Future

This is your best weapon in resolving conflict in the workplace, especially when you are dealing with aggressive or passive-aggressive individuals. They will often find it appealing to not have their actions examined and brought back into the discussion. Leaving things in the past and focusing only on solutions allows both parties to put aside their anger and frustration and exchange it for the calm exchange of ideas on solutions to the problem.

Go Into the Discussion Prepared for Solutions

You absolutely must go into difficult discussions armed with possible solutions. It is important to let the other party weigh in with their own opinions, and the solution you find together may not resemble any of the options you put on the table at the beginning of the meeting.

But, when you go into the situation prepared to collaborate for solutions, and you have a few to offer, it shows that the other party can have good faith that you are going to be fair in your handling of the situation.

At the same time, thinking about potential solutions before the confrontation will give you the opportunity to ensure you have rebuttals for any arguments the other party brings into focus, as well as the opportunity to consider points on which you will refuse to budge.

Chapter 7: Resolving Conflict After It Starts

Even if you handle everything perfectly, there are some situations that are guaranteed to end in conflict. With all the measures you can take to ensure that your message is clearly understood, and options are provided, the ball is in the other person's court. If they refuse to work with you or keep their own temper in check, a confrontation is bound to happen.

It is also possible that you are enduring workplace conflict now, and that is what prompted you to read this book in the first place. If that is the case, you're going to need to understand how to apply this knowledge after conflict has started to rear its ugly head. The goal is to resolve conflict in a calm, rational, and amicable way that subverts emotional outbursts or physical confrontation.

Effective Conflict Resolution Strategies

Conflict resolution strategies must be tailored to the specific situation, including the cause of the conflict, the potential root problem of recurring conflict, and/or the individuals involved in the conflict. Without examining all sides of the scenario, you will not be able to develop an effective conflict resolution strategy. On the other hand, most strategies will fall into a few common categories.

Remember those conflict management styles we talked about in chapter four? As we discussed then, not all these conflict management strategies should be applied. However, most situations can fall within three conflict management styles: compromising, accommodating, and collaborating. Each of these management styles has its own related conflict resolution strategies.

Collaborating Conflict Management Style

You should use the collaborating conflict management style with its corresponding conflict resolution strategies whenever possible. **Collaborating is not the same thing as compromising!** It is extremely important to understand this distinction.

When you compromise with someone, you are giving in on some points while getting the other party to give in on other points. They say that a good compromise is when neither party walks away completely happy. But this is exactly the problem. When you compromise, everyone loses. When you collaborate, everyone wins.

Collaboration is quite different. When you collaborate with each other to come up with a reasonable and equitable solution to the root issues involved, both parties win, even if they don't get everything they wanted when they came to the table. Collaboration allows parties to work together to come up with solutions that incorporate all perspectives and recommendations of the situation and parties involved.

Here are some collaboration conflict resolution strategies you can use in real world situations:

- Maintain an atmosphere of mutual respect by remaining polite and straightforward. You do not want to be blunt or without tact, but you do want to be very clear and forthright. Being upfront and honest will go a long way toward finding the problem at the heart of the situation and collaborating to solve it.

- Look at the big picture. Approach this as an opportunity for organizational or policy change rather than an opportunity to resolve conflict. You may be successful by resolving a conflict directly in front of you, cooling off tempers and resolving the immediate problem. But without making changes that address the root problem first, any conflict resolution is temporary and will only last until the next frustrated outburst.

- Take responsibility. In almost every situation, each party can identify at least one way in which they reacted or behaved poorly. Consider the situation carefully and recognize your part in the conflict. Verbally take responsibility for your involvement in the escalation of the situation. This lets the other party know that you see both sides of the situation and are truly looking for an amicable and reasonable solution to the root problem.

Unfortunately, there are some situations in which collaboration is not possible. If you need a quick solution to an immediate confrontation so that business needs can be met in the short-term, you may need to take a more decisive action, such as forcing the issue or being completely accommodating on a temporary basis.

For collaboration to work, both parties must be willing to:

- Commit to finding a mutual solution. This means finding the root of the problem and addressing it amicably from all perspectives.

- Schedule plenty of opportunities for discussion to find win-win solutions. Finding a solution to the root issue that benefits everyone and takes all perspectives into account takes time. But even if you must use another strategy on an immediate basis, there is great value in returning to this method.
- Everyone must maintain trust in each other's desire to reach a cooperative solution that meets the needs of all. Selfishness and stubbornness have no place in collaborating conflict management styles.

The clearest benefit to using the collaboration conflict management style is that you will be building a foundation for resolving conflict in the future. In fact, as mutual trust and respect is built on both sides through collaboration, workplace issues can be identified and resolved reasonably before conflict or confrontation ever become an issue.

Of course, it takes effort to engender a spirit of collaboration and camaraderie. Everyone is human, and you may find yourself becoming frustrated or impatient while you manage a particular conflict. If you find your temper getting short and falling into the forcing or compromise conflict management styles, you should take these steps to bring the situation back to a spirit of collaboration:

- Make sure you understand the situation from all sides and perspectives. If you aren't sure, ask probing questions and listen for understanding rather than to respond.
- Offer possible solutions that will benefit both parties.
- Be honest about what is and isn't possible in resolving the conflict.

- Get commitment from all involved to ensure that everyone is on the same page and ready to resolve the conflict amicably.

Occasionally you may find that to come to an amicable agreement, both parties must step away from the conflict to maintain composure. It is natural for two sides involved in a deep or complex conflict to be somewhat emotional. Tempers can flare, which is why it is so important to remain calm, assertive, and fair in your assessments and solutions.

There is no shame or harm in pausing a conflict to resume negotiations and resolution later when both parties can be calmer. It may also be helpful to have an unbiased third-party mediator help you communicate more effectively to collaborate for equitable solutions.

Compromising Conflict Management Style

If you don't have time to get to the root of a problem and search for a win-win solution, you should definitely consider taking the time to at least compromise with the other party to reach a temporary solution. Compromising involves both parties being willing to give and take according to their needs and desires.

They say that when you compromise everyone comes out a loser, and that is definitely true. Compromise isn't about finding solutions. It is about making each other happy enough to continue going about your day without affecting the rest of the business that needs to occur.

Compromise can also foster or escalate feelings of competition and spite, which can lead to unreasonable conditions to the compromise that serve no purpose other than to make things difficult for the other person. Still, when you are in a time crunch and just need everyone to get back to work, compromise can be an effect resolution style.

Here are some of the conflict resolution strategies that correlate with this resolution style:

- Make it clear that this compromise does not take the place of true conflict resolution. It is very important that all parties agree to come back to the table to collaborate on potential solutions at a later date, even if that date is not currently decided.
- If you are not going into the compromise with an actual date and time to pursue a win-win solution, you should at least provide a date and time by which such information will be provided. Make sure you follow up, or your word means nothing and you're down to being accommodating or forcing.
- Separation is often the best conflict resolution strategy to employ quickly. As part of your compromise, agree that you will remain separate until such time as the root problem can be identified and addressed. Since compromise usually ends with both parties frustrated and angry, separation can help prevent further escalation of the issue, including physical confrontation.

Of course, there are some downsides to compromising with someone who is being unreasonable. You may not be able to use compromise to resolve an immediate conflict if:

- One or neither of the parties are willing to back down from their demands.

- The parties are not likely to meet their end of the compromise without close supervision and force.
- Trust is already shaky between the parties, and compromising will only create a competitive environment that breeds more conflict.

If you are unable to compromise with someone, and the conflict must be resolved quickly and without actual confrontation, you may find yourself needing to be either forceful or accommodating instead. These two extremes should be used only when other methods of conflict resolution have failed. While the compromising approach isn't necessarily the best overall, it is the best option when an issue needs to be solved immediately and there isn't time for collaboration.

Avoiding conflict management style

As mentioned earlier, there are two primary ways to get out of a confrontation immediately so that you can avoid the problem, at least temporarily. These two extremes are to be completely accommodating, or to be forceful in policy or chain of command. Either strategy should only be used as a stopgap to halt conflict or confrontation until such a time that the root problem can be addressed. Which strategy you use depends on the situation and your role in it.

Accommodating conflict resolution strategies

Accommodating conflict resolution strategies are based on giving the other party exactly what they want in exchange for their cooperation in continued business activities. If using this approach, it should be made clear that the accommodation is only temporary and will be replaced with a more reasonable solution beneficial to both parties.

117

Generally, you should always try to compromise when you need an immediate solution so that you can maintain your position while the other party feels that they won on some level. This gets everyone back to work with the least amount of hard feelings. But when that isn't possible due to a lack of trust on either or both sides, accommodating might be the only way to get someone back to work without causing a confrontation.

However, there are some instances in which you should not be accommodating to someone that is causing conflict. When giving someone what they want causes any type of harm to the organization, department, team, or an individual, you cannot in good conscience accommodate them.

In general, you should not be accommodating when:

- Giving into demands would be hazardous to the reputation of the business or others in the department.
- Giving into demands would be detrimental to the careers, well-being, or mental health of another individual or "bystander"
- Giving into demands would violate law, company policy, or both.

It can be very tempting to be accommodating to immediately resolve conflict, especially when the person causing the conflict is aggressive or passive-aggressive, and you are concerned about their reaction if you push the issue. Unfortunately, this is usually when you must fall back on the forceful approach.

If you are in a position of authority, and you do not have the time or resources to pursue true conflict resolution in the moment, it may be necessary to take an assertive approach. Doing so likely means reminding the other party of your authority and making it clear that they must perform their job as required or face consequences based on human resources policy.

Again, it is important to be clear that this is a temporary solution, not the end of the conflict resolution process. Making sure that the other party knows you plan to address their specific problem at a more appropriate date can go a long way toward diffusing a mounting temper, even if they are just doing what they are told in the end. To ensure another conflict needing immediate attention doesn't arise, you should follow up swiftly with details on how you plan to collaborate to resolve the core problem.

Start by Assessing the Situation

Before you can decide on the best conflict resolution strategies to use in the moment, you first must get an accurate assessment of the situation. While you may need to make split-second decisions if the confrontation is already heated, use all the time you can make available to get to the meat of what is going on according to all sides, even if you are in the middle of the conflict.

What is the Perspective of Each Party?

Not everyone can practice empathy but making an attempt to see the perspectives of others can give you a lot of insight into how to deal with a particular situation. Knowing where each side is coming from puts you in a better position to collaborate to find solutions to the problem. It may also help you understand your own role in the conflict, and how you might make changes to prevent conflict in the future.

Recognize Your Interpretation of their Behavior May Not be Accurate.

While it is true that body language, tone, and verbal cues can all play a role in communicating thoughts and feelings to others, it cannot be used as the sole basis for interpretation of someone's motives. Although most people cross their arms when they are closed to suggestions and being stubborn, others cross their arms to stop fidgeting when anxious. We could list many more examples of exceptions to the body language rules we all learn through interpersonal communications.

The bottom line is that you are not a mind reader. You do not know what that person thinks or feels, or why they do what they do. Not unless they tell you. If you believe you know what someone's behavior or body language is telling you, ask probing questions to determine if you are right rather than operating on assumptions.

Back to Active Listening Skills

When you use active listening skills, particularly asking follow-up questions for understanding, it will give you a different point of view with which to consider the situation. Asking questions designed to better understand the situation from all sides is a vital step in the collaboration conflict management style. Continuing to ask questions based on answers will quickly get you to the root of the problem and some possible solutions.

Resolve Misunderstandings with Clear, Accurate Information

So often conflict is the result of a simple misunderstanding blown entirely out of proportion, or a minor conflict leading to major repercussions that can ripple throughout an organization. When a misunderstanding is the root of a conflict, resolving that misunderstanding is often the only step needed to completely solve the matter.

Refute Inaccurate Information with Facts

If the other party keeps firing "facts" at you for which they have no basis, or may be mistaken, it is important to respond respectfully rather than with accusations. For example, if someone is adamant that a particular policy applies, but you have evidence that it doesn't, impart this new information in a respectful and polite manner that will garner attention.

Some people are prone to accusing others of being wrong instead. While the individual may, in fact, be wrong in their own assumptions or recollection of facts, stating so only fuels the conflict. Responding with irrefutable fact is the only logical course of action.

Keep the Focus on the Situation, Not the Parties Involved

It's easy to point fingers and say "That's not what I thought you said," or "You didn't make that clear." Again, even though

121

these statements may be true, it is counterproductive to state such, especially during an already heated conflict.

Instead, keep the focus on the issue at hand. What is the truth of the situation? How does that truth stand up against the perspective of all parties, individually and together? What is the heart of the matter, the original problem that led to the conflict? Addressing these situational questions keeps misunderstandings from becoming heated confrontations.

Taking Responsibility

Taking responsibility for your part in creating the conflict is extremely important, and it can shape the continuation of the interaction. Resolving conflict after it starts is much easier if you agree that you played some role in the situation. Taking responsibility doesn't just mean apologizing. It also means implementing some of these conflict resolution strategies:

- Shift the focus from who is right or wrong and onto differing perspectives. Agree to disagree in the spirit of resolving the issue once and for all.
- Thinking of it as one side against the other, especially if you are a third party to the conflict, is only going to create a battle mentality. It is better to think of things as being fair to both parties.
- It is easy to jump to the defensive, but owning responsibility means empathizing with the other parties involved in the conflict. If you played a part in the conflict, that means the other person has at least one valid point.
- Taking responsibility means not pointing fingers, even if there is one person mostly to blame for the situation. Instead of playing the blame game, accept the situation

for what it is and focus on collaborating to find solutions.

- When you take responsibility for your part in the conflict, you are more likely to put your brain into problem-solving mode rather than trying to win an argument or battle of wits.

A verbal apology can go a long way, but when it comes right down to it people need to see for themselves that you are taking responsibility for your actions. That is why the above strategies are so important. Behaving in these ways shows the other person that you are serious about finding a mutual solution.

Offering Support When Needed

Sometimes conflict is borne out of a person's frustration with a particular situation or project. Many people don't know how to ask for help or support when they need it. Some may even feel that asking for support in the workplace is a sign of weakness, and that it should be avoided at all costs. After all, isn't it better to work out the problems for yourself to show initiative and competency?

Not necessarily. When it comes right down to it, asking for the support you need in the workplace can be well worth the effort if it prevents future conflict. If asking for assistance with a project, task, or difficult situation can prevent the anger and frustration that leads to conflict, why wouldn't you do so? The obvious answer is that, regardless of the type of support you may need, you should be clear about your needs to your colleagues and supervisors.

And the same is true when you put the shoe on the other foot. When you see someone struggling with a project, task, or situation, and it is clear they could use some help in resolving the matter, offering such support can deescalate a situation so that it doesn't ever become conflicting or confrontational.

Recognizing When Someone Needs Support

Since most people don't like to ask for help, it is important as a supervisor or managerial employee for you to understand the signs of someone needing assistance. Sometimes you can recognize and offer exactly the right support without ever speaking with the individual. Other times, you will need to actively engage with them and ask probing questions to determine the problem to be solved.

The most common signs that someone has hit a wall and needs support include:

- Decreased productivity or decrease in quality and performance of work duties. If someone who is normally productive is suddenly the opposite, they probably need assistance of some kind to move forward.
- Suddenly displaying poor work ethic, such as tardiness, excessive breaks, or calling off from work.
- Out of character, unprofessional and/or inappropriate speech, including inappropriate language, cursing, yelling, or bullying.

Anytime you see a colleague or subordinate struggling to complete tasks as usual, it is an indication that there is some type of issue to be addressed. Although you may not be able to resolve all the problems that can lead to such performance issues, it is likely that directed conversation controlled with probing questions can give you an idea of the type of support needed by the employee.

Sometimes people just need a brain break and may need the rest of the day off in order to come back at it tomorrow with fresh eyes. Especially when people are collaborating on a project, feeling frustrated or temperamental can be detrimental to the project, and some time away can be very sobering.

Types of Support for Clients

When clients are on the verge of conflict, either with yourself or others within the organization, those customers are often looking for a specific type of support to meet their goals or needs. Whether they feel that their service or the product was not as expected or they are unhappy with the level of customer care, the following actions usually resolve most support needs:

- Take responsibility for your part or your organization's part in the problem and avoid mention of issues brought on by the customer's behavior or reactions, unless those actions voided a contract or warranty.
- Product and service support, so that the customer knows exactly what the product or service is supposed to do, which may resolve issues with what is actually occurring. This might involve supplying detailed product information, instruction manuals, or troubleshooting guidelines.
- Use empathy statements and avoid unproductive facial expressions or body language, such as those that can be mistaken for humor or mocking.
- Don't offer your opinion, agree with them, or disagree with them, but rather make the situation clear with

facts about the circumstances, products, and services in question.

- Ignore angry comments and focus on an equitable solution.

While it is important to recognize and meet the needs of your customers, it is also important that you do not violate company policies or procedures to satisfy them. There is a difference between offering support and engendering a spirit of collaboration and accommodating someone to give them what they want in direct opposition of an equitable conflict resolution.

Types of Support for Colleagues

Have you noticed that one of your colleagues has suddenly shut down rather than being their usual bubbly self? All conflict can leave someone unprepared to deal with the work at hand, even if it has nothing to do with the workplace. While you do not want to get involved in the personal lives of others, there are some things you can do to support coworkers going through personal or work-related conflict.

- Third party mediation for parties to resolve the base conflict causing the workplace difficulties. Essentially, the mediator is there simply to keep things civil and the conversation productive, while the colleagues work out a solution to the conflict on their own.
- Guidance to reference materials relating to the conflict, including company policies or organizational standards. These might include the employee handbook or code of conduct, as well as other training documents.

- Research into all sides of the situation for a clear overall picture that can be used to find solutions to the problem.

If you see a colleague or subordinate struggling in completing their work when they are normally very good at what they do, don't be afraid to ask them if there's something you can do to help. While you may not be able to accommodate their initial request, it can open up a dialogue that can help them resolve their issue before it affects the workplace with resulting conflict.

Types of Support for Subordinates

If you have subordinates that seem to constantly be in the middle of workplace conflict, it is possible that the employee needs some additional support to be successful in their role. Some subordinates who take on additional responsibilities or supervisory tasks as part of an implied or direct promotion are not adequately prepared and therefore do not have the tools necessary to be successful without conflict.

It is best to address these situations from a standpoint of looking for the root problem so that it can be corrected. If workplace conflict is occurring frequently around the same sticky points, these issues should be addressed directly utilizing established company policy and an attitude of mutual respect.

Before jumping into disciplinary measures, work with the subordinate to determine the exact reason that they are involved in the conflict, and how the conflict started. That can often give significant clues as to the best way to resolve the conflict so that it doesn't continue to occur in the future.

Another thing to remember is that sometimes people need to perform tasks hands-on before they can grasp the nuances of a position. This means that some people may not get as much out of initial training until they perform the task. When such is the case, the employee may simply not have retained the information, and need additional training or a refresher as to the duties of the job in which they are struggling. Often adequate training and coaching in policies, procedures, and expectations can resolve conflict quite effectively.

Collaborating to Come Up with Solutions

Some people say that collaborating is the same thing as compromising, but that just isn't true. Compromises end in lose-lose situations in which no one is happy, and few needs are met on either side. By contrast, collaborations end in win-win situations that take into consideration the needs of everyone involved.

For collaboration to take place, time needs to be blocked off for in-depth deliberations. All parties will need to be available to discuss all aspects of the situation, coming at it from all sides to determine a fair and equitable solution for the good of all. That usually requires several meetings to discuss how things got to this point, and where to go from here to move forward and meet the needs of the organization.

Be Prepared to Both Offer, Receive, and Adapt Solutions

There is almost always more than one way to tackle a problem, and rarely will one solution meet every need of the circumstances. The most successful conflict resolution strategies are those that favor the needs of the many over the needs or desires of the few. This means that you must be willing to vary your views of possible solutions to meet those of your colleagues.

Go into the meeting with solutions already in mind. You should have more than one to offer, and the more potential solutions you put on the table the better the other side will believe a truly just resolution will be reached.

You should also be ready to accept solutions from others involved in the situation. In fact, you should outright request possible solutions from all parties, especially during the first meeting or discussion. Asking others for their input as to what the root problem is and how it should be resolved also lets them know that you expect them to participate in conflict resolution, not just sit there and be told what to do.

Once solutions have been put on the table by all parties, it is best if everyone is able to adapt their solutions to incorporate elements from others. In this way, everyone can work together to come up with a fair solution that addresses the needs of all.

Be Prepared to Negotiate

Even though collaboration and compromise are two different things, they can both involve negotiation. Unfortunately, few conflicts are resolved with both parties getting everything they want. Even though you are working together for a win-win solution, both sides are likely to make concessions to make the solution work for all. If you go into the discussion with the intent to stubbornly refuse negotiation, you will not be able to successfully resolve the conflict, at least not long-term.

Be Prepared to Bring in Others to Help Solve the Problem

Sometimes the people involved in a workplace problem are too close to it to find a reasonable solution. When that happens, it may be necessary to bring in others to work out a solution. As mentioned earlier, a third-party mediator can be a great option to keep discussions in check and productive. You can also make use of subject matter experts from other departments. Depending on the nature of the conflict, you may also want to involve your human resources team.

The bottom line is that you need to involve anyone in the organization that is going to be beneficial to finding a solution to the current and future conflicts.

Chapter 8: Common Workplace Conflicts and How to Resolve Them

A rmed with all this information, you should be able to resolve most workplace conflicts without too much difficulty. However, it is helpful for many people to be able to apply their newfound knowledge to real-world situations. As such, we will spend the rest of this book going over how to cope with the most common workplace conflict.

How to Deal with Passive-aggressive Communicators

Perhaps the most difficult people to deal with are those with a passive-aggressive communication style. Passive-aggressive individuals are almost always listening to respond, giving little care to what you want to speak with them about, or their role in any conflicting situation. They are only interested in what affects them personally.

You can't converse with a passive-aggressive communicator the same way you would, say, a passive speaker or an assertive speaker. Because they will try to turn everything around on you, it is important to choose your words wisely. Here is some important information on how to recognize passive-aggressive people and how to approach them in different scenarios.

Recognizing Passive-aggressive Behavior

Passive-aggressive people usually think that they are hiding their negative thoughts, attitudes, and emotions well. In reality, anyone paying attention to what they are actually saying can tell that these individuals are not interested in mutually beneficial conversation. In fact, they may be perfectly fine with a negative result for themselves if it was also an inconvenience to the other party.

Some of the behavioral clues that passive-aggressive people exhibit include:

- Denying anger, frustration, or other negative emotions, even though their language clearly shows that they are reaching a boiling point.
- Baiting others to cause flares in temper or frustrated/angry outbursts, then pretending they were blameless in the incident.
- Appearing completely cooperative, but rarely following through.
- Venting on social media to avoid direct confrontation while still displaying their anger.
- Constantly making excuses, usually while also putting the blame for their actions square on the shoulders of anyone else on whom they can pin it.

It is also important to note that **gaslighting** also falls under the passive-aggressive category. Some people are better at hiding their aggression than others. Those that can remain completely outwardly calm are often prone to gaslighting. To gaslight someone is to turn the conversation around to intentionally confuse and/or anger them to make them appear they are being irrational, or to make them think themselves irrational.

Gaslighting is very abusive, and it falls through the cracks in monitoring abusive behavior in the workplace. Individuals very good at passive-aggressive communication use gaslighting every day to start or continue workplace conflict, often without notice.

Ignoring Aggressive Undertones

Aggressive undertones are the hallmark characteristic of passive-aggressive communicators, and you should be able to spot them easily. Even though most of these individuals think they hide it well, it is usually easy to pick out the common phrases that indicate aggressive undertones.

"I'll get it to you--" Making promises for pushed deadlines with no intention of making good on them is a classic passive-aggressive tool, and one that is easy to miss if you aren't paying attention. It usually takes a few interactions with someone before you catch on that these promises are sure to go unfulfilled.

For the most part you should take notice of aggressive undertones, but do not verbally acknowledge them. In fact, it is best to show by your body language that you didn't catch the aggressive comment at all, even if you did. This will throw them off balance, and they may rethink their strategy.

Usually passive-aggressive people are communicating that way because they already see a conflict, and they don't want to be the one to pull the trigger on a confrontation, even while their anger is seething just beneath the surface. They are saying these aggressive things because they are trying to get a rise out of you. If you ignore the comments and move forward with the conversation, it completely disrupts their thoughts and actions.

If you ignore these aggressive comments and undertones, one of two things is likely to happen. Either the other person will shut down, seem accommodating, and may or may not follow through, or the individual will become angry that you are not taking their bait, and they will lead the confrontation anyway.

If you know you are going to be having a difficult conversation with a passive-aggressive person, make sure that you have someone with you. This is a necessary precaution, both for a witness in the event of a confrontation and/or backup for your arguments.

Understanding Motivation

One of the biggest keys to dealing with a passive-aggressive person is to understand their motivation. If someone doesn't normally display passive-aggressive behavior, their use of the passive-aggressive communication style may be situational due to their own thoughts and/or emotions. Knowing why someone is behaving a certain way is key to determining the root problem that needs to be addressed before progress can be made.

There can be many different reasons for someone to suddenly seem passive-aggressive, or to be using that communication style out of the blue. Some of the most common reasons that people are passive-aggressive in a conversation include:

- Fear of losing control of their temper due to bottled up frustration
- Anxiety over things that are beyond their control, but affect them in a big way, such as a performance metric.
- Low self-esteem causing them to put all the blame on themselves, even as they really believe that someone else is responsible for the problem.
- Lashing out defensively, seemingly for no reason, or jumping to the defense due to conclusions based on

their own guilt, even as they are angry about being blamed for the problem.

As you can see, passive-aggressive people are very complicated, and rather contradictory at times. It is important to listen carefully to the aggressive comments within your conversation for clues to their motivation for their behavior. Once you know their underlying motivation for their aggression, you can deduce the core problem so that it may be addressed once and for all through collaboration.

How to Show Empathy Instead of Aggression

It is easy to become frustrated when talking to a passive-aggressive person. They will stick to their ground even if you prove that they are wrong, and they will intentionally ignore your meaning to be obtrusive. In the end though, "tough love" is not the way to go.

Instead, you should show as much empathy as you can, especially with someone that is naturally passive-aggressive in their usual behavior. Many people who are abused or neglected, either as children or as adults, become passive-aggressive because they are afraid of losing their temper and being rejected in some way because of it.

Often passive-aggressive communicators don't even realize that they are using that communication style at all. They may think that they are being straightforward about their needs and vexation, but they are really afraid of speaking out on their own behalf. That fear can sometimes add fuel to the anger, which can make it volatile. If you are dealing with such a person, it is important to be openly empathetic and reassuring. Pointing out the behavior can also put a stop to it in these instances.

Clear Presentation of Possible Solutions to the Root Problem

If someone is being passive-aggressive, they are probably also going to be rather argumentative. When you try to address an issue, they are likely to shut down or lash out defensively, shooting down any solution you offer up for examination. They will make it very difficult for you to even get out all the details of the solutions that you are proposing.

To avoid this impasse, it is important to go into the conversation with several possible solutions depending on circumstances and unknown variables. Be prepared to defend those solutions to the teeth, and know how to present them in the simplest, fastest way possible so you can get in the details before you get shut down or the brick wall goes up.

It is even better if you can weave these solutions into the natural conversation as rebuttals to their aggressive comments, but that may not always be possible.

How to Deal with Aggressive Communicators

Aggressive communicators are only better than passive-aggressive communicators in that they do not try to hide their aggression. As such, it is much easier to spot and easier to contend with an aggressive personality or communicator.

Again, if it is not natural for this person to be aggressive, you should try hard to find the motivation for the hostile behavior. This will give you a big clue as to the actual issue at hand so that it can be addressed head on and avoid any future conflict.

Regardless of typical behavior, someone who is acting combative or confrontational should be handled delicately.

You need to make sure that you are being firm in your position without further flaring tempers.

What are the Most Common Traits of an Aggressive Communicator?

Aggressive communicators are easy to spot. When someone has an aggressive personality or has reached that level of anger, they are beyond trying to control their outward appearance and attitude. Some of the most common signs of aggressive communicators are:

- Trying to dominate the other parties in the conflict, seeking a win-lose solution and making issues unnecessarily competitive.
- Giving unconstructive and vague negative feedback or criticism when approached about their own performance.
- Raising their voice, sometimes unintentionally, as their temper rises.
- Interrupting frequently so that they can continue their rant instead of finding solutions.

In addition, you may occasionally find yourself needing to deal with aggressive people who resort to shouting, swearing, and sometimes physical displays of anger that can cause property damage or personal injury.

It is best, of course, to avoid such situations as much as possible. If you find yourself in this type of situation, avoid each other until you can meet with a third-party mediator to discuss the real issue beneath the surface.

How to Cope with a Bully

Some aggressive people will do their best to demean you, confuse you, heat your temper, or otherwise mentally or emotionally control you. Even though you don't really see very many instances of physical confrontation in the workplace, these verbal altercations can often be just as damaging.

To deal with a bully that continually acts as the aggressor, even when it is not clear why, you must start by setting a limit as to how much you are willing to take. Decide this limit for yourself, because you cannot set and keep a boundary with an abuser if you have not committed to that boundary for yourself.

Once you have made that decision, relay it clearly to the workplace bully, being certain that they understand what you will do if they cross the boundary or don't stop the harassment. Document everything, even if it seems minor or petty. It all adds up in the end. When you reach that point that you set for yourself, stop trying to reason with the bully and go to your supervisor or human resources department.

If you are dealing with the average aggressive person, you can try these tips to maintain control of the situation:

- Remain calm, even if the aggressor tries to "push your buttons."
- Clearly state your feelings, needs, or desires using "I" statements.
- Recognize that the aggressive individual also has needs and seek to understand them so that they can be met. Make it clear that this is your intent in the process to make them more agreeable and cooperative.

- Approach escalating tempers with empathy and basic human respect.

We discussed additional strategies for dealing with conflict with an aggressor earlier in the book. Bullies are simply aggressors that often don't know how to express their needs or the underlying issue at hand, so they lash out in anger and frustration. As a reminder, some of those key conflict resolution strategies for dealing with aggressive communicators are:

- When possible, have back-up and present a united front on the issue at hand.
- Make sure that you are seeing the situation from all sides so that you can get an unbiased perspective and find a reasonable and amicable solution.
- Keep control of the conversation by continually bringing it back on topic.
- Use "I" statements to passive-aggressively bring attention to the hostility you are feeling in the room without putting any blame on one person.
- Stand your ground and be firm in your resolutions. Be flexible enough to come to a mutually agreeable conclusion but stand your ground when it comes to the things most important to you.

One of the best things you can do, in addition to the above, is to adopt an attitude of caring and empathy. When an aggressor recognizes that you truly understand where they are coming from and that you are truly willing to collaborate for an amicable solution, they are much more likely to calm down and collaborate for a long-term solution, even as you stand your ground.

Sharing and Receiving Criticism

One of the most difficult conversations to have with someone is a poor review or critique of their work. Unfortunately, these conversations must happen on a regular basis for individual career growth and the growth and support of the organization. Without the giving and receiving of criticism within the organization and outside of it, there can be no progress.

There isn't one particular way to address all occasions of giving or receiving criticism. Everything depends on the parties involved, the type of criticism needed, and the expected outcome of the conversation. (Such as if someone will be disciplined for their actions.) It is necessary to assess the situation first to determine the best approach.

How to Give Constructive Criticism

Whether you are giving someone criticism over a particular piece of work or coaching them on overall performance, telling someone their work is not up to par is not something anyone wants to hear. You must decide going in as to the appropriate conflict resolution strategies based on what you know of the person.

If someone knows that they are about to receive an evaluation or appraisal of their work, they are likely to start out being on the defensive. That means that they are likely to listen to respond with a defense rather than to really understand why you are critiquing them. Surprise them into listening by thanking them for their contribution to the organization or department before jumping into the reason for the discussion.

The most important thing to remember is that you want to give **constructive** criticism. What makes criticism constructive? It must provide feedback that can be applied to foster improvement. The biggest problem with most critics is that they only tell a person what is wrong, rather than telling them what they need to do to change it.

The purpose of criticism in the workplace should be to coach team members to become more productive and successful members of the organization. When companies and managers put the success of their team first, organizations thrive.

Of course, you are always going to have those few people that are stubborn and jump to the defensive regardless of what tact you try to take. When that happens, it will be impossible to impart wisdom until the individual has calmed down.

Be accommodating at first, letting them vent their defense. When they seem to be finished, agree with them on points where you can, and use these points to lead into the criticism you needed to impart in the first place. By taking this approach, you may find a natural way to improve performance without having to provide outright or outspoken criticism.

How to React to Constructive Criticism

Everyone finds themselves on the side of receiving criticism at some point in their careers, no matter how well they perform their job or know their industry. Everyone makes mistakes. It is important that you make sure you are responding to criticism appropriately. Consider the difficulty that the other person may be having in confronting you with the poor evaluation, since you will be able to see the situation from both sides.

Also consider how you would hope a subordinate of your own would respond to your constructive criticism. Try to behave in the way that you would expect of others.

If the criticism is not constructive and is merely negative commentary with no feedback for improvement, it is natural to feel angry and confused, especially if you don't usually receive negative feedback. Give yourself a few moments to consider your response by taking a few deep breaths. Instead of being defensive or confrontational, ask for more information.

"What, exactly, was the issue with--" Repeat the critique back to them, verbatim if you can.

"What could I have done differently?" This is also a good option for gathering more information to get constructive feedback. Using open-ended questions that appear to be in agreement with their evaluation is a perfect example of the accommodating conflict management style.

"Do you have an example of what you are looking for?" This is another example of an open-ended question that could save you both a lot of time and frustration. Sometimes people just don't know how to explain what they need. Asking for an example puts you both on the same page.

Of course, there are a lot of ulterior motives that might influence someone's feedback. When that happens, it may be impossible to get more information about what was wrong with your work, simply because there was no mistake made. When someone is criticizing you and it doesn't seem to be making sense, it is probably because they are doing so in retaliation.

If you are dealing with such a situation, it is best to use the avoidance conflict resolution style on an immediate basis. You will not be able to reason with such a person on your own, because their very argument is unreasonable. Contact a superior, another colleague, or someone from human resources to mediate as you use the collaboration conflict management style to put an end to such petty disagreements.

Resolving Insubordination

One of the most common workplace conflicts you will run into is insubordination. Once you reach a supervisory level, you will be responsible for ensuring that employees are performing their job duties as expected. If one of those employees defies you or company policy outright, they must be dealt with promptly.

How you deal with insubordination can set a precedent for how you will respond to insubordination from others in the future, even if you don't intend for it. But employees talk to each other, and if you don't handle the problem appropriately it could backfire on you. You must address the insubordination firmly while still being empathetic enough that the rest of the staff doesn't turn on you. It can happen much more easily than you might think.

Instead of jumping to write-ups and other disciplinary action, try using the following strategy to manage insubordination without confrontation and while avoiding conflict.

Discover the Root of the Problem

It is true that sometimes insubordination is borne from a natural tendency to challenge authority or a general dislike of a supervisor. However, most of the time insubordination can be traced back to one incident that they feel was handled poorly. In a way, insubordination is passive-aggressive behavior at its finest.

As such, you're going to use some of the same strategies that you would use with any passive-aggressive communicator. That includes discovering the root of the problem. What actually triggered this behavior? Discovering that million-dollar question will lead you to the solution to put an end to the insubordination once and for all.

Unfortunately, most passive-aggressive people don't feel able to communicate their angst effectively. The reason they are passive-aggressive is that they do not feel comfortable having open discourse with others, so they act out their frustrations in a way that they hope is subtle (but rarely is). That means getting them to open-up and tell you the root cause of the conflict could seem to be nearly impossible.

To find the root of the problem, begin the conversation by asking probing questions. Start by pointing out the behavior or performance failure that led to the conflict, then ask them if they can explain why it happened or what caused it. From there, you can ask probing questions as they make sense.

Some great starting questions could be:

- Why do you think that happened?
- Is there something that (name or department) could have done differently to better the situation?
- Did you have a better solution? Did you bring it up? If not, why not? If so, how was it received?
- Do you have a solution in mind to resolve this conflict?

If asking these questions does not get a helpful response, you must do additional research to figure out what caused the conflict with this individual. Try to look back at previous interactions, as well as recent behavior. These might give you clues as to what started the conflict, and how it might be resolved. You can then go back to the individual and ask more probing questions. You may repeat this process a few times before you get to the root of the problem.

Identify Possible Solutions for Improved Behavior

Before you meet with an employee about their behavior or job performance, you should be well prepared with some potential solutions to improve conduct. You may need to adjust based on the conversation or interview, but you should have several "what-if" scenarios in mind going into the meeting.

When you bring up solutions to improve performance, do so in such a way that it appears more like a partnership between you to make each other and the company successful rather than in a way that makes them feel they are being admonished like a child. This will go a long way toward getting their attention and getting them to work with you on a solution.

Don't forget to ask them what their solutions are, or if they have a reasonable excuse as to why the behavior changed/happened.

Be Honest and Straightforward

It is normal to be anxious when you must talk to an employee about their insubordination or poor performance, and when you are nervous it is natural to take on a meeker attitude and tone. As such, you may not be as clear or straightforward as you need to be. It is important that you maintain confidence, hold your head high, maintain eye contact, and be clear about expectations and next steps.

If you fail to make it clear what behavior was unacceptable and what is expected to happen to correct the problem, you cannot fault them for non-compliance. If you want anything to change, you must be honest and direct about the unwanted behavior and how it should be corrected.

Document Everything, and Try to Have Witnesses

If you know that you are going to be dealing with a passive-aggressive employee due to decreased job performance or outright insubordination, you should do your best to have at least one witness to the conversation.

This is extremely important from a human resources standpoint. If you do not follow HR policy, keep records of any coaching conversations or disciplinary actions, and have evidence of your interactions, you open the door to expensive and time-consuming HR issues that are bad for business.

If you give any type of disciplinary action, even if it is just a "verbal" warning, you should get the employee to sign an acknowledgement so that there is no question later.

Resolving Conflict with a Supervisor

Just because they are in a higher-level position than you are doesn't mean that they are blameless. Supervisors and managers are just as capable of causing workplace conflict as subordinates and entry-level professionals.

Dealing with such situations, however, can be quite dicey. You must be firm and stand up for yourself, but you must do so in a productive way that cannot be misconstrued as misconduct.

This requires a calm and reasonable collaborative conflict resolution management approach.

Clearly Communicate Your Position

The first step in getting something done about your problem is making sure that the right person knows a problem exists in the first place. Go to the appropriate person in the appropriate position within the company and clearly communicate the problem from your perspective. Do not be opinionated or offer solutions at this point. You should simply state the facts, and why they are constituting a problem.

Once you have stated the problem, you need to make them understand your position on the matter. How is this problem affecting you? What can you do about the problem on your own? What do you need help with in this matter? Do you have solutions that work with cooperation to resolve the root issue?

Providing all of this information about the matter that is troubling you ensures that the other side of the conversation knows exactly what you need and why.

Actively Listen to the Problem from the Other Perspective

Especially if you are bringing up a problem you have with a basic policy that the company or department follows, you're going to need to understand the situation from all sides to collaborate for a suitable resolution to the conflict.

After you have stated your case, be prepared to really listen to your supervisor and their side of the matter. There may be nuances to the situation of which you are unaware, and upon discussion it may become clear that there may be other obstacles and variables at play.

If your supervisor doesn't seem to agree with you, but also doesn't seem to be offering any valid reason for their disapproval, ask probing questions to try to find out why. Once you know why they have reservations about the issue, you can address them appropriately in a reasonable and calm way.

Present Solutions and Be Open to Other Resolutions

The best way to approach any conflict is as a problem solver. Going into talks with your supervisor armed with solutions, shows them that you can solve issues without assistance, and that you can adapt as needed. It also shows your supervisor that you are aware of the problem at hand and are already seeking ways to solve it.

Be Honest if You Need Support

Everyone needs some type of support from their supervisors. Even if you are a very independent worker and prefer to rarely see your direct supervisors, you still probably have some type of requirements for your workstation or environment, scheduled hours, etc.

Unfortunately, it's not always easy for people to identify when they need support, or what type of support they need. And, even if you can identify what support you need from your supervisors, most people find themselves unable to speak up on their own behalf. Still others simply don't know what to ask for, and because of that they ask for nothing.

But your supervisors should be there to help you succeed, whether that means training and coaching to improve skills or accommodating an unavoidable personal issue. If something on your end led to a conflict with your supervisor, letting them know exactly what is going on could help them determine and meet your needs, even if you are unable to put words to them yourself.

Personal issues that may require support

While all professionals strive to keep their careers and personal lives separate, there are some situations in which you may have personal needs that affect your ability to perform your job duties adequately. While employers cannot meet every personal need and issue that might arise, there are some problems that may be able to be addressed with a bit of support from management. Some of these may include:

- An acute medical condition that requires temporary disability accommodations
- A non-work-related injury that requires temporary accommodations
- The acute or newly chronic medical condition or injury of a child or senior in your care that will require you to actively participate or provide transportation for ongoing medical treatment
- Divorce, a death in the family, or a terminal diagnosis causing emotional turmoil, leading to decreased concentration, attendance, and performance

Of course, not every employer makes their employee needs a priority, even if they are work-related. When the root of a conflict is a personal issue, some managers may refuse to even listen to your needs and accommodation requests. When this is the case, you should talk to your human resources department or upper management. There may be policies or procedures in place for getting such support. In fact, you may be able to get more support than you could have hoped by simply letting the right person know about your situation.

Work-related issues that may require management support

Occasionally there are generally work-related issues that could affect your performance and/or lead to conflict with a supervisor. Even when these situations have nothing to do with your supervisor directly, bringing the issue to them may help you resolve it.

Some common workplace situations that can cause conflict with management include:

- Inability to grasp a new task, procedure, or piece of technology necessary for adequate performance of the career position
- Difficulties with other employees, even if they are from other departments, especially when they affect your ability to collaborate for a successful outcome
- A hostile or abusive work environment created by fellow colleagues or employees, even if they are not in your department
- Minorities feeling as though they are being passed over for promotions and raises due to discrimination, but can't prove it

And as always, some companies can be filled with poor management that couldn't care less about their employees' welfare. Not only will these supervisors fail to assist you in succeeding in your position and career, they may intentionally sabotage it. In those cases, it may be impossible to get the support you need. If the support you require is related to discrimination, harassment, or bullying of any kind, you should seek other remedies to the problem, such as talking to the company's human resources department or filing a complaint with upper management.

Fielding Conflict with an Unreasonable Supervisor

If your supervisor has violated your code of ethics, civil rights, company policy, or federal, state, or local laws and ordinances, you will likely be unable to reach a resolution with them on your own. It is also impossible to reach a resolution to long-term conflict if your supervisor seems to be retaliating for reasonable and legal actions (i.e. whistle-blowing). It is also improbable that you will receive any assistance from supervisors that appear to be discriminating against a minority group or personal dislike.

For immediate conflict resolution with management such as this, it is usually best to accommodate your supervisor, when doing so does not break law, your code of ethics, or company policy. While it may anger you even more to concede in that moment, it is usually for the best. Going to another department or manager to report the issue for a longer-lasting resolution isn't a practical solution in the heat of the moment.

From there, you can contact your human resources department or upper management, as company structure allows. These individuals will be much better equipped to resolve the ongoing conflict in a permanent and reasonable way. Through such collaboration and compromise, you may be able to work out your differences with the supervisor. Often these situations will end with the employee or the supervisor moving to a different department or position.

Conclusion

Having completed this book, it should be very clear to you that conflict resolution isn't just about solving arguments in the workplace. There are many different types of conflict, made more difficult to navigate by different types of people. Everyone is different, and sometimes two people just cannot communicate effectively.

If you find yourself in the midst of conflict, or potential conflict, and you're not sure how to respond, it is best to get advice from someone else familiar with your organization's culture and policies. You can reach out to someone in your human resources department, your own immediate supervisor, or other management personnel as required by the situation.

Finally, remember that conflict can start with you just the same. Be mindful of your own actions, thoughts, and behaviors, and ask for help if you need it before a conflict starts or worsens. Other ways that you can become more effective in conflict resolution include:

- Continue your education with philosophy, psychology, or management courses that teach you how to read people and situations.
- Watch conflict resolution on the sidelines, especially when there is a master communicator at work. Just make sure you stay out of the way of fire.
- Implement workforce development programs within your organization to teach others how to be mindful

of their words and actions, and what to do to prevent conflict in their department.

As with anything, conflict resolution skills improve the more you utilize them. Practice these skills, not just in the workplace, but in every area of your life for the best results. Eventually you will be a master at communicating with others on their level and preventing conflict before it ever arises.

Good luck!

CPSIA information can be obtained
at www.ICGtesting.com
Printed in the USA
BVHW050554250223
659177BV00012B/968

9 781955 423120